Charlie,
To an old friend and
classmate. It was wonderful
to see you again.

Ron Harper

THE HARDER I WORK, THE LUCKIER I GET

THE HARDER I WORK, THE LUCKIER I GET

CONVERSATIONS WITH
RON HARPER

A
MEMOIR

PRESERVING MEMORIES
Charlotte, NC

Preserving Memories
Charlotte, NC
www.preservememories.net

ISBN: 0-9742576-2-1

LCCN 2004094075

2004

To my longtime friend, sweetheart, and lifetime companion, my wife of over fifty-two years,

Katherine

Table of Contents

1979 Ron at work in our old Crompton Street office
"Unposed–honest!"

Ron Harper

1932   Born December 3 in Oldtown, Maryland, to Myrl and Dolly Harper

1950   Graduated from high school, then immediately entered the U.S. Marine Corps

1951   Katherine graduated from high school, then began full time work with the Bank of Charlotte

1951   Met Katherine in Wilmington, NC. She was 17 years old, Ron was 18. Katherine was a bank teller. Ron was a Sergeant in the Marines

1952   Married February 12. Now have 5 children and 13 grandchildren

1952-1971 Worked for Charlotte Textile Engravers and Consolidated Engravers

1971   Founded Ron Harper Associates, Ltd.

1975   Changed name of company to Harper Corporation of America

1978   Founded Harper/Love Adhesives Corporation

1980   Founded Harper Machinery Corporation

1989   Sold Harper Machinery Corporation to brother, Dick Harper

1997   Opened Harper Corporation Division in Green Bay, Wisconsin

2000   Licensed anilox technology to Ruam Zub, Bangkok, Thailand, to form Harper Asia/Pacific; HarperScientific™ Division created.

2001   Harper GraphicSolutions™ Division began

2002   Celebrated 50th Wedding Anniversary, February 12, at the Renaissance Suites Hotel, Charlotte, N.C.

2004   Founded Harper Graphics, a Harper/Inometa Company" in Germany

Preface

As I have reflected back on my life during the last ten years, I have consciously wondered what it is that makes Ron Harper tick? Why have I always been in such a hurry? Why am I often not satisfied once a goal is reached or an objective achieved? I have felt if those questions could be answered then just maybe I could slow down and "smell the roses" a bit more.

What I have increasingly realized is much can be learned from examining the work ethic I learned early in life and have stuck with throughout my life. Encapsulated in this ethic are the values that gave me the persistent motivation needed to succeed in business. To better understand the relationship between my attitude toward work and the way I have lived my life is what I set out to do in putting this book together.

I don't play the lottery or engage in any kind of gaming, legal or illegal. Yet, if for some unforeseen reason my name was picked out of a hat and I was informed I had fortuitously won ten million dollars, I would have a very difficult time accepting the winnings. I just wouldn't feel right about it. I'd have to refuse it or give it all away to some charitable cause.

Over the past thirty-three years, since my wife, Katherine, and I founded Harper Corporation of America, we have been fortunate to have accumulated a considerable estate. But even if someone had given me ten million the day we were married, fifty-two years ago, when we had little more than the clothes on our backs, I have this feeling it would have been dreadful for me. Not that we didn't struggle financially at times. There were periods early in our marriage when I was unemployed and still needed to provide for a family with five children. The point is we can look back over all those years of getting to where we are today with a feeling of satisfaction. Had the results of those fifty years of hard-earned success happened overnight, I would be a different person today. I think life would have been terribly unfair to us if all of our success had come to us without a lot of hard work.

In my mind, I have always associated work with pride in accomplishment, personal dignity and an overall sense of well-being. Getting the prize—some big windfall—without any effort would seem totally out of line to me. Golf pro Gary Player once said, "The harder you work, the luckier you get." I feel like I would have been deprived of the best part of life if I had not had to spend my life working for what I have.

In the pages that follow I tell my life story, beginning in a little manufacturing town in Maryland during the Great Depression. Given that my career pursuits have been such a significant part of my life, I try to trace the development of my work habits. From the example of my hardworking parents, to my time in the U.S. Marine Corps, to my early employment experiences, I have sought to understand how it is that I learned to be so devoted to the work I do. Much has to do with the role models I learned from. Being given responsibilities I was not fully prepared for, struggling to overcome feelings of inferiority, and having a burning desire to succeed shaped my character as well.

The accumulated experience I gained early in my career while manufacturing and marketing rollers for printing presses gave me the confidence needed to found Harper Corporation of America in 1971. Since then, our company has become a leading supplier of anilox rolls used in flexographic printing presses, with an international market. We can also claim credit for some of the more significant innovations in flexography over the past thirty years. We have seen flexography rise from being a low-quality, less-expensive type of printing to where it now competes with offset printing in full color and is quickly gaining market share.

In addition, I delve into how my own business practices have been shaped through the course of my career. My strength has always been in marketing and sales and I outline here the tactics I have used, as well as my management style. The final two chapters focus on the rewards Katherine and I have experienced in giving back to the community some of the profits we have garnered, and my own reflections on a lifetime of fulfillment arising from a career that I truly fell in love with.

My father died at age sixty-five. Dad was not a talkative person. He seldom expressed his feelings or discussed what was on his mind. I learned little about what life was like for him growing up as a young West Virginia farm boy, his career, his hopes or his dreams. No question about it, I loved my father, but I never really knew him well. And I miss that intimate, more defined connection with my past.

I also admit that as a teenager I probably would not have been interested in hearing Dad tell me about having to ride a horse to school through two feet of snow, or about his tough life on the farm, or the difficulties our family faced during the Great Depression. Now I am interested, and unfortunately, it is too late to ask him for answers that are so important to me. The other reason I wanted to write this book is to answer questions about me, for my family. Answers that some family members may have no interest in at the moment, but in time, they will. I hope those who read this book will enjoy doing so.

I have dedicated this book to my longtime friend, sweetheart, and lifetime companion, my wife of over fifty-two years, Katherine (Katherine Tessie Hodges prior to our marriage). Ours was a teenage marriage that did succeed, mostly because of the patience, forgiving ways, and perseverance of Kat, as I am fond of calling her, or "Babe" or "Doll." The latter, coincidentally, are the same endearing terms I often heard my father use when talking with my mother—which, strangely, gave me a feeling of warmth and security.

Katherine has been my supporter, mentor, motivator, wife, and lover for these many years, even when I probably deserved less. I have not always understood Kat, but I have always loved her dearly—and will until the day I leave this earth. As Katherine has often heard me say, "We have had a wonderful and happy marriage—most of the time—for over half a century."

I also dedicate this book to our wonderful family—our children, sons-in-law, daughters-in-law, grandchildren, and great-grandchildren—and to friends who may be interested in "what makes Ron Harper tick." I thank them all for their love, support, and friendship. I will be forever grateful.

An added thanks to four very special people who most influenced my adult life. I regard them as the *four most influential people in my life*: my mother; my high school typing teacher, Mrs. Livesey; Katherine, my wife; and Al Scala, my boss in my early working years, who mentored me like a son. These are the role models from whom I gained confidence and often received undeserved support as I struggled to "find the real me" in a sometimes unfriendly and competitive world. I happily give credit and address each of their unique contributions in this book.

Last, but not least, my sincere gratitude to Jack Nelson, who assisted me with my personal memoirs—for without Jack, this book would probably not have been written—and my personal thanks to MaryEllen Goodwin and Sonya Long (Harper Corporation of America Marketing Department) for their special help in compiling the photographs appearing in this book.

CHAPTER ONE

My Early Life

I can actually claim to have been born in a log cabin, in Oldtown, Maryland, about 120 miles west of Baltimore. My father grew up on a farm in West Virginia and at age sixteen moved to Maryland to take up employment at a large chemical manufacturing plant in Cumberland, known as Celanese Corporation of America. My mother grew up in Oldtown, but left when she was fifteen and moved to Cumberland, about ten miles northwest of Oldtown, and went to work in a hospital as a nurse's aide. She was seventeen when she met my father, who was just four days older than her. Dad was born on May 5, 1913, and named Myrl (pronounced Merle) Lonnie Harper; and Mom, Dolly Marie Dolan, was born May 9, 1913, during the presidency of Woodrow Wilson and a year after the *Titanic* hit an iceberg and sank.

Mom told the story about how shortly after Dad had given her an engagement ring, they were in his car and he put his hand on her knee. She responded by slapping him in the face. He said, "Doll, we are going to get married soon," and she said, "We aren't married yet," threw the ring out the window, and got out of the car. I was their first child, after they worked out their differences and were married, at age eighteen, in January of 1932, the height of the Great Depression. People who lived through the Great Depression remember 1932 as the year the Lindbergh baby was kidnapped. Herbert Hoover was president.

My birth occurred on December 3, 1932. My mother's sister, Florence, and her family lived in an ordinary house in Oldtown. Behind it was an old log cabin where my parents lived for a while after they were married. I was born there. There was probably a midwife in attendance, but I was never told any more—and didn't ask. I really don't recall any other details about the old cabin.

My name, Ronald Lee, was chosen by my mother. Ronald Coleman was my mother's favorite movie actor and that is where the Ronald came from. As a suave gentleman, he starred in early silent movies like *The White Sister* (1922) and *Beau Geste* (1926), then, after sound was added, in *Bulldog Drummond* (1929 and *Arrowsmith* (1931). He was even better known for his later performances in *A Tale of Two Cities* (1935) and *Lost Horizon* (1937), among many others. My grandfather, who died when he was thirty-three, was named Lee Harper, and that is where the Lee came from. I was known as Ronnie up until my second real job, when I was about twenty-eight. At that point, thinking Ronnie sounded kind of childish, I began introducing myself as Ron.

The family name Harper has Scottish roots and is occupational in origin. In my understanding, the name is derived from the Old English word "hearpere" and denotes one who played the harp. In medieval society, the harp held an extremely important role, and from early times a harper was a hereditary official in the household of influential families.

We moved to Cumberland shortly after I was born, the first of about a dozen moves during the time I was growing up.

Cumberland was very much a blue-collar town—a "big city" to me—of about twenty thousand people. The railway industry dominated the place. The Western Maryland Railroad ran through on one end of the downtown section, and about three or four blocks away on the other side, the B&O Railroad passed through.

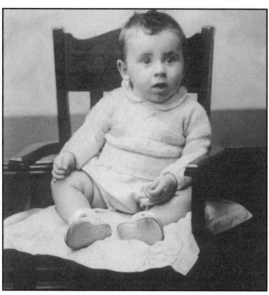

1933 Ron Harper, six months old
"Already seriously contemplating my future"

They had their respective yards where railway cars were sorted to make up the trains. I was a kid during the age of coal-burning steam engines, so it was not unusual to see billowing clouds of black smoke coming out of the smokestacks on the old locomotives. I recall, in my bare feet, crunching the cinders from the coal soot on the concrete sidewalk. If a woman hung washed clothes out on a line to dry and a train came through with black smoke billowing out, the smoke ended up on the clothes. We never thought much about all the pollution because the railroads meant jobs and people earning a living.

Many of the industrial buildings and the downtown structures in Cumberland were built in the late 1800's and early

1900's. The breweries were a big part of the local scene. We had the Queen City Brewery and Old Export Brewery. Beer was definitely the preferred drink and people drank a lot of it. Other important industries included Celanese Corporation of America, employing thirteen thousand people and located a bit out of town. Kelly Springfield Tire Company was also there, as was the Cumberland Steel Mill. The largest employer in Cumberland was Celanese. The second largest was Kelly Springfield Tire Company.

The Great Depression that began in 1929 had a merciless grip on America throughout my childhood and, no doubt, shaped my outlook on life in both conscious and unconscious ways. The importance of work, both as a means of livelihood and as a source of personal dignity, was an all-important value I learned growing up. Employment was generally pretty good in Cumberland up through World War II, due to the heavy industries. But I can recall the deep strife that sometimes flared up between the unions and management.

My work values, however, were probably shaped more by my parents. Up until I was about thirteen, my father remained steadily employed at Celanese, working his way up to a position as a supervisor, a white-collar job. He took his job very seriously. His sympathies were non-union when he had a job there. A couple of times the union pulled strikes at Celanese, and Dad had to work. He actually lived out at the plant for a month or six weeks at a time because supervisors had to keep the equipment running, with police outside the gates to control the union picket line.

In addition to my dad's employment, from the time I was very young, my parents operated a small grocery store at one locale or another. The grocery stores were generally run out of the front room of whatever home we were currently living in. The first three stores they had were in the house, and the fourth was kind of a beer parlor/grocery store, with gas pumps out front. That fourth one was probably five miles from home.

Neighborhood families maintained little gardens in their backyards and grew vegetables, lettuce, turnips, and maybe potatoes to supplement their food supply, but they would buy their meat, beans, and such at our local grocery store. Dad might buy a twenty-four can carton of peas and another carton of twenty-four cans of something else at a distribution warehouse. People would then buy these items from Mom and Dad one can at a time. And though there was home delivery of milk, we had milk in the store. The milkman stopped outside the store every day and dropped off eight quarts; so if neighbors were short on milk, we had it in glass bottles.

Being in the front room of a home, these stores were smaller than today's convenience stores. Unlike the latter, the shelves were stocked mainly with essentials rather than junk food. The one exception was what we referred to in Cumberland as "tonic." Tonic was Pepsi-Cola, Royal Crown Cola, and Coca-Cola. (I never heard it called tonic anywhere other than Cumberland.)

When the store was in the front of the house, Mom had a bell on the door so she could go back and throw some clothes in the washer, start dinner, and that sort of thing. People would come in and call out, "Hey, Doll, are you back there?" and she would come out and wait on them. Maintaining the store consumed much of her energy. Dad generally would help out when he got home from his Celanese job and they would keep the place open until seven or eight at night. Later they had, what I refer to as, the "beer joint," down the road from where we lived. The beer joint would stay open until eleven at night or midnight. At that location, one door would lead into a beer parlor and another to the grocery story, and there were gas pumps out front. Dad worked all day and then he would close the business with Mom at night, and they would come home after that.

For me, during the time I was growing up, there wasn't a big divide between the world of work and private, home life. It all kind of went together. People worked, and the more they worked the better off they were. Dad made fourteen dollars a week at Celanese during the Depression, which was a good salary at the time. But my folks no doubt saw the financial problems other people had and the desperation some people faced. Having the grocery store business was an added source of security. Putting in long hours working was a big part of their lives, and Dad never felt confident enough to leave his day job and just help Mom keep the grocery store going.

I don't remember much about those early years. My brother Dick was born seventeen months after I was born and he became my closest childhood companion. Once he was out of the crib, we shared a double bed, right up until I was seventeen and left to join the Marines. People today may find that a bit strange, but in those days it was common for siblings to share beds in small, overcrowded homes. I do recall Dick and I drawing pictures on the walls in our upstairs bedroom with crayons when I was about five years old. We couldn't understand why Mom got upset about it. They were pretty pictures, we thought, but she got somewhat disturbed.

For the most part, however, my mother was a tremendous source of comfort and security for me as a child and up through my teenage years. I felt very attached to her. As a child, every winter, probably for the first ten to twelve years of my life, I suffered from earaches. I had many more than other children. All I knew was I got them, and Mom would put hot oil and cotton in my ear, and hold me close so I could feel the warmth of her body. That closeness was soothing, and the earache would go away.

Memory of my relationship with my mother is most poignant when I think of my first year of school. I can remember the fear of going to school. I had to leave home, had to leave Mom. Standing at the bus stop, waiting, and feeling the insecurity set in is something that remains vivid to me. My insecurity was all internal. There was no crying and no real reason for my feelings

"Looks are deceiving. I was the Innocent one."

1937
Ron Harper   Dick Harper

1940
left: Dick Harper
right: Ron Harper

except for Mom being absent. I got accustomed to attending school but never forgot how important my mother was to me.

Other than my fear, my early schooling experience was rather positive. I loved my first grade teacher, Miss Taylor. To me she was an old lady, probably in her late twenties or early thirties, but she was the motherly type and made me and the other kids comfortable.

The school was Columbia Street School in downtown Cumberland. A two-story structure, built of brick, it was probably thirty years old when I started there. To a little kid the school seemed like a big place, with ten or twelve steps leading up to the front entrance. I imagine the building had about twelve classrooms, and I attended first through sixth grade there.

I remember I enjoyed school. I struggled for my grades, or felt like I was struggling. The Cs came easy; the As and Bs I had to work harder for. I was satisfied at the time to be average. The only strong incentive I had was praise from my mother, but I don't recall Mom or Dad being particularly concerned as long as I got Cs or Bs on my report card.

I was more of an introvert at that stage of life, not so much a loner, just shy, someone who didn't mix easily. I think my shyness was why I felt more comfortable at home, where I didn't have to mix and I wasn't among strangers. Still, I do remember the little notes teachers used to write on our report cards. Positive remarks were important to me. The one I most remember is when the teacher commented saying something like: "Mrs. Harper, please talk with Ronnie about not talking when others are talking." That comment kind of contradicts my being an introvert. Apparently I would chatter at times when others were participating in class.

Our family continued to grow. My sister, Joyce, was born when I was six years old. And Gary, the youngest in the family, was born when I was ten. Mom somehow kept up with the grocery business and taking care of all us. Meals at home were simple affairs. I was raised on meat and potatoes, so to speak. We used to eat a lot of hamburgers, something we loved and Mom readily fixed. She could prepare them in a hurry while keeping an ear out for the door opening in the store. I learned at an early age to fry hamburgers myself and make hotdogs, but I never learned much else about cooking. Like a lot of kids, I never really enjoyed greens. Spinach I can tolerate, but vegetables in general, I have to make an effort to eat. I don't recall Mom ever encouraging us to eat our vegetables.

Mom did all the cooking and baking at home using a woodstove in the kitchen. She used to say it was the only way to cook. She cooked on the woodstove long after electricity was available in places like Cumberland. It was years later, when I was around twenty, before Mom got her first electric stove, and even then the stove sat in a room by itself for a while because she refused to use it. She said food just didn't taste the same as it did cooked over a woodstove. She was even slower converting from the old-style washing machine with the ringer rollers to a more modern spin washer and dryer. Mom was just slow in making such changes.

Sunday noon meals were frequently a little fancier: chicken and mashed potatoes, maybe, or beans, corn bread and meatloaf. Mom used to bake cakes and pies, and make home-made ice cream. I ate a lot of desserts as a youngster. That is something I have always loved, and still do, though I'm not addicted to desserts the way I was for many, many years.

Sunday afternoons we would sometimes travel to the lake and go swimming and maybe have a picnic. Dad went along because Mom twisted his arm. I think he would have rather done something else. A meal out for us in those days would be going down to what was referred to as the Coney Island Restaurant, where vendors served hotdogs. People usually wore long-sleeved shirts year around, and a guy would have a pack of cigarettes in his rolled-up cuff. There in the restaurant, the fellow behind the counter generally had his shirtsleeves rolled up well above the elbow. He would line hotdog buns up all along his arm and then take the wieners and throw one in each bun before adding mustard or whatever. This was in the days of no air conditioning, so there had to be more than a little perspiration on his arm. Of course, we thought nothing of it at the time, and the hotdogs were wonderful. Pizza and Chinese food I didn't experience until after I was married.

Holidays were celebrated in modest yet meaningful ways in our household. Christmas was the biggest event for us. My parents would never go buy a tree but would go out in the woods and find the prettiest tree they could find, cut it down, and take it home. At home we would place it in a stand and trim it, often staying up late Christmas Eve getting it all done. My brothers and sister would have to go to bed on Christmas Eve and then Mom and I would decorate the tree. As for gifts, we never got a whole lot, but we were always given more than oranges and apples, which is what my mother received when she was a kid. A memorable Christmas, of course, was like when we were given bicycles. Dick and I got bikes when we were still young and rode them everywhere.

Thanksgiving was probably the next biggest annual holiday event for us, generally accompanied by a big family get-together. Easter was celebrated in like manner. I don't remember celebrating birthdays, however. There were no gifts given out on a person's birthday. Birthdays were not a big event in my mind until after I got married and learned new traditions.

Religion wasn't a significant influence in my early development. Mom certainly was a God-fearing person, but neither she nor Dad attended church much. The exception to this was when I was around six years old; for a brief period, we went to a Nazarene church not too far from home. Dad probably just tolerated going for the sake of the family. Someone once told me a good Italian father makes sure his family goes to Mass every Sunday. He may not go himself but he makes sure his family gets there. For that brief time, my father, though he wasn't Italian, took the position of a good Italian husband and father and made

26

sure we got to church. Mom and Dad liked the pastor. I enjoyed attending Sunday school and recall at Christmas the church gave us oranges. The church folks liked to organize picnics and other fun events kids enjoy.

Then one day the young pastor came into our grocery store and spotted the cigarettes and chewing tobacco for sale. He, certainly with good intentions, made it clear to my parents that they were going to have to quit selling that stuff, because it was sinful. His pronouncements didn't make Dad too happy. I don't think he ever went back to church again in his life. In the end, the results of Dad wanting to set an example for the family was we came to understand that going to church wasn't important. Mom would occasionally take us kids to church after that, usually at Christmas and Easter time, but church was not big on our family's agenda.

I was always fearful of my father. He was a muscular guy as a young man, though not because he did a lot of outdoor, physical labor. His stature was average, but for some reason he was well built, and he was a good-looking fellow. He was not foul-mouthed like a lot of working-class men were in those days. I never heard him say the word "hell." Typically, if he was angry, he would say "dan-it." The worst word I heard my dad say was one time he said "bastard," and it shocked me. Mom cussed like a sailor at times, but my father never did. Nonetheless, to me he was a frightening presence. He'd bark and we would sit up straight. When Mom would say, "Wait till your daddy comes home," I'd listen. I don't know if Dad ever really spanked me or gave me reason to be afraid of him, but I just was afraid of him. He may have cuddled me as a baby but as a youngster and a teenager my father never gave me a hug that I remember. You didn't do that kind of thing if you were raised in West Virginia. It was not very macho to do so.

My mother was different. She had had a difficult childhood. Her mother died when she was three years old. She

Myrl L. Harper
"My Dad."

could remember sitting on her father's lap when her mother
was upstairs very ill. They had an enclosed stairway to keep
the heat downstairs. As Mom was sitting on her father's
lap, they heard what sounded like a boulder coming down
the steps and hit the door at the bottom with a big bang.
Mom remembered her father just saying her mother was

Dolly Marie Harper
"My Mom."

dead; and she was. Her father, my grandfather, remarried to a lady named Kate when Mom was probably about five years old. The kids all hated Kate. So my mother and her brother moved in with one of their older brothers and his wife. My mother didn't exactly get the best of care in that household. Yet, despite the traumas of childhood, Mom

29

developed a positive outlook on life and completed nine years of schooling, one more than Dad completed.

I remember Mom always being vibrant and excited and positive. She loved to play the piano and sing, playing "by ear," as she called it. She later told me that back when she first met Dad, she used to perform on the radio. She was singing on the radio and working at the hospital. After they married, Dad said he didn't marry a "Paula parrot for the public," so he made her quit. Her singing career was gone, but she would still sing at gatherings and was always the life of the party, which Dad seemed to admire and appreciate.

There were times when she would be ironing and singing. She seemed to have been a very happy, take-life-as-it-comes, sort of person. I always admired her. She was the kind of person people liked to be around. She made people feel good, not necessarily by what she said to them but with her upbeat attitude, always smiling. People would come to Dolly if they were going to have a party; and if there was a piano available, she would play and they would all get to singing. Mom would tell the jokes. I don't recall my father ever telling a dirty joke, but Mom would, more with women than in mixed company unless it was a couple she knew well. She was just that way. She was someone others looked to for fun or associated with because they knew they would have a good time.

Mom was short, about four feet eight, and had a problem with weight most of her life. When she was thirty years old, a doctor recommended she begin smoking to curb her appetite, and she did. From the time she was thirty until she died at eighty-four in 1997, she smoked.

Home life was constrained in many respects by the work habits of my parents. At the time it all seemed normal to me. My mother was kind of the head of the household. Dad may have been the boss, the one who worked long hours at two jobs. But Mom got her way at home. She was always there for us and we always knew we could rely on her. There was never any question that she loved my siblings and me.

My father and mother were hardworking people, with an above-average income because of the number of hours they put into their work and the kind of risks they were willing to take. They owned two cars during an era when most families living in towns and cities did not have a car, and when, in the rural areas, people could barely afford one. Even as a child I could see what other people accomplished versus what my parents accomplished and realized they had done something more with their lives. They were average people, all the same. They didn't flaunt their success.

The example of their work habits and, particularly, their conviction that people can better their lot in life through disciplined work had a deep and lasting impact on me and was probably the most important lesson I learned from my parents. I became determined to succeed like they had succeeded in bettering themselves. I also resolved early on that I wanted to do it in a white-shirt-and-tie job. I felt like I deserved it. A white shirt and tie to me were signs of accomplishment. I don't know where this attitude came from, but I began thinking of myself surpassing my parents' achievements. I felt like I wanted to do something more and I was capable of doing more. All I had to do was work harder than most people to make it all happen.

When I was thirteen, a dramatic shift occurred in our family life. Our dad wanted to introduce us to farm life. He felt we needed the change, and it was important to him. So my parents made a down payment on a seventy-five acre farm near Fort Ashby in West Virginia, ten to twelve miles due south of Cumberland. Dad could still commute to his job at Celanese and we could all get acquainted with life on the farm. I don't think he really intended to make a living off the farm and I don't think his intention was to teach us to want to

May 1943 Ron Harper, ten years old; sister Joyce,
four years old; brother Dick, eight years old
"Not quite ready for church."

grow up and become farmers. Part of his thinking may have been him wanting to get back to his own roots. Being on a farm may have reminded him of when he was a kid, country living, farm animals, and all that. He just wanted to introduce us to the farm environment. I remember we moved the year President Roosevelt died, 1945, and Harry Truman took over as president, then World War II ended.

For us kids, particularly Dick and I, the move seemed like a good idea. The farm was fun, at first. Looking at our new life from the outside, we had these animals and all this open space. We moved into a log house renovated by the previous owner. Though built out of logs, the house was not as rustic as you might think of when imagining a log cabin. But it wasn't fancy either, like some contemporary log homes.

There were just two rooms on the first floor, a large kitchen with a woodstove for cooking, and a small living room. Upstairs there were three small bedrooms. In some ways, the cabin was a better place than homes on the neighboring farms. This house had indoor plumbing and, whereas most people did not have electricity and relied on kerosene lanterns in the evenings, our new home had a dozen Delco batteries in the basement to power a lighting system.

Joyce would have been seven or eight at the time and Gary was only three or four, so most of the responsibility for looking after the animals and taking care of other chores fell to Dick and me. We had two horses, three cows, about six pigs, and probably seventy-five chickens to look after. But the romance of our new life quickly wore off. We hated feeding the chickens, and the pigs aggravated us. The cows were okay except at milking time. The horses, we loved.

The farmer next door plowed up the ground for Dad and planted corn. Our job was to hoe the weeds around the growing corn. The task could become unbearable in the summer heat and when the corn got high enough to hide behind, we would take off for the swimming hole in the nearby creek. Dad would keep reminding Mom, "Get those boys into the cornfield." In the early summer, our job was to gather the hay, a job we particularly detested. Again, a neighboring farmer cut the hay for us, but this was before there were hay bailers. We had to go into the field with a horse and wagon and pitchforks and pitch the newly cut hay into the wagon. We'd then pull the wagon up to the barn, and pitch the hay up through a door into the loft, with all the dust and crap coming back down on us. It was hot, itchy work. We knew the job had to be done and we did it; we just didn't like it.

During that period of time, I developed some pretty strong ideas about what kind of work I wanted to do in life. Admittedly, I became a bit of a snob. I also resolved I would never own a pickup truck, and I never have. Most of the farmers drove pickup trucks. Dad drove one and loved it; though his was in better condition, not the rusty, beat-up variety we saw so much of in West Virginia. I guess in my mind I equated pickups with the kind of jobs I didn't want. I became convinced I did not want to grow up and become a farmer. I, also, did not want to be a back yard mechanic. I did not know exactly what I wanted to be, but I wanted to do something more with my life.

It wasn't long before Mom and Dad got back into the grocery business. They bought, or leased, I'm not sure which, a place in Fort Ashby. Again, it was one of those beer parlor-type places, a grocery store on one side and a parlor where drinks were served on the other side. Out front there were gas pumps. The business kept Mom busy during the day and sometimes into the evenings. Dad would come home from Celanese and go directly to manning the bar and gas pumps. Dick and I were left to look after the farm.

We had to attend school in Fort Ashby as well. The experience was okay. We attended a small school and I made a lot of friends. All of the students were, to some degree, coming in off the farm. There was not a lot of pretense, like there sometimes was in the Cumberland school. The clothing we wore was not a big issue. Even as a kid, though, I realized something was lacking as far as my education went. I don't know that I totally appreciated the importance of education, but I knew there ought to be more than I was getting. The worst example was one science teacher who used to have us silently read a chapter to ourselves during class and answer the questions at the end of each reading section and then turn them in. While we were doing that, she sat in the front of the room behind her desk, turning the pages of a comic book in her lap.

I went out for basketball at school and couldn't even make the team, a team that lost every game they ever played. I decided I was not cut out for sports, and I never played softball, football, baseball, or any other kind of ball on a school team.

We had been on the farm for almost two years when, shockingly for us kids, our parents separated! Dad took off and went to New Mexico or somewhere else out west and was gone for two or three months. Mom carried on at the grocery store, but the family income fell dramatically without Dad's paycheck from the chemical plant. It was a scary time for me. I was left with a confused, insecure feeling, not being sure what was going to happen the next day—a frightening experience.

When Dad finally returned, Mom and he reconciled. I don't think she ever let him forget the incident, but she still loved him. The matter was never discussed with us kids. We were just happy to see them back together.

Life for us took another dramatic turn soon afterward. Mom and Dad sold the farm and the store in Fort Ashby and we moved back to Cumberland. The farm had been fun and exciting, with many new experiences, but we kids were delighted when we moved back to Cumberland. My parents rented a small house near the city dump, a less-expensive area to live in. I remember when we first moved in the smell was horrendous, but after a while we got used to it. We lived there about a year, in 1947, before my folks could afford something better.

Meanwhile, Dad had lost his job at Celanese when he separated from Mom and left to go out west, and when we moved back to Cumberland he couldn't find a job. He ended up taking a job in a steel mill in Baltimore. As it was about a 140-mile commute, he stayed down there during the week and came home on the weekends. He wouldn't accept any charity or public assistance. A bit later, he found a job with the railroad.

During the twenty years Dad worked at Celanese, he would refer to the men who worked on the railroad as "those dirty railroaders," even though he did have a respect for them. In those days they were dirty. When they would take their caps off, everything from their foreheads up was all white, and everything below the cap line was black, because of the coal dust and smoke. Well, Dad ended up being a railroader, and he stayed there for thirty years, and loved it.

He started out as a brakeman, then was promoted to fireman, shoveling coal into the engines. When the diesel engines came along, the firemen really were not needed any more, but the unions forced the railroad companies to keep them. So their job basically was to make sure the engineer stayed awake. Dad eventually took a test and qualified to be an engineer, which among railroaders is the ultimate position to have. He always was on what they called the "extra list." As an extra he had to fill in for other engineers, but that didn't mean he only worked occasionally. He stayed plenty busy. The railroad had a "caller," a dispatcher, who might telephone him at two in the morning, and say, "Hey, Myrl, we have a freight train leaving in the next hour and we would like you to be there." He would get out of bed and grab that freight train. Or, he might, at three or four in the morning, jump on a passenger train and "deadhead" down to Baltimore as a passenger and then engineer a freight train coming back. He was always on call.

Mom was soon back in the grocery store business, running another operation out of the front room of our home. By that time, Dick and I were old enough to be expected to contribute to operating the business. We used to help stock the shelves when new supplies arrived and, increasingly, helped customers in making their grocery purchases. Much of the customer shopping was done "on time," as we called it. If you were a customer of ours, you might come in, or send your children in, to get a can of evaporated milk and a half pound of minced meat and three or four eggs. And if I was on duty, I would make a note on a pad like waitresses carry, little "tickets," we called them. The pad would have the customer's name on it, and I would make a note of the cost. If the customer was someone's kid, then we knew the parents, and the parents knew us and trusted us. When payday came, they would come by and settle up their bill.

By that time a large A&P supermarket had opened in town. Supermarkets were new in the 1940s and not always easily accessible for many people. This one was seven or eight miles away for folks on our side of town and many of them did not own an automobile. People would try to get to the A&P about once a month to stock up on staples. They might borrow a car or go with a neighbor and load up. Most of what people bought in our neighborhood store was "fill in." Although they could put together a meal from what was available, it was much more expensive.

My relationship with my mother remained close. She was a talkative person and shared a lot with me in a way she might talk with a neighborhood friend. I appreciated that. She didn't share much about her marriage or real intimate matters. But she treated me like someone who she could confide in.

Mom always looked at me as the oldest child, which I was, and I felt her expectations for me were higher. I generally had chores to do that my siblings were not old enough to assume responsibility for. Even as they grew up, Mom continued to expect me to take responsibility for many tasks most of the time. She gave me a reputation to live up to, more so than any of the other children. I think they sensed this and I may have appeared to them to be her favorite. I'm not sure their assessment was altogether true, but I can understand why they might have thought so. Mom was the first one who really had faith in me. She always had more confidence in me than I had in myself and was always pushing me and encouraging me. My mother was the *first significant role model* in my life, and I relied heavily on her

1947 Ron Harper, 9th grade–fourteen years old
"When I had a little more hair."

for emotional support even as I grew older.

I think most of the early moral values I acquired in life I learned from my mother. She taught me not to steal or speak badly about people. Just about everything accurate I ever learned about sex, and it wasn't much, was from my mother. She was concerned that I learn to be respectful of girls, and made it clear to me that the worst thing that could ever happen was for a girl to get pregnant out of wedlock. Her sister got pregnant back in the 1920s. She never talked about the episode much, but I still got the message. Most of all, she taught me a general outlook of honesty and fairness.

Somehow I developed a belief that eventually I would have to pay for everything I get, so there is no use taking shortcuts or living in hopes of a lucky break—or I'd feel like I didn't deserve the good fortune. What's more, I feared that down the road I would have to pay it back or make up in some way for it, because there really is no getting something for nothing. Better to pay for what I get up front and know what the costs are rather than get some benefit and be uncertain of when and how I am going to have to pay for it. Uncertainly still scares the hell out of me. The predictable part of life is what I learned to respect, while I feared the uncertain. Honest work was the predictable way to pay for what I got, and I learned to persist in my efforts to get what I wanted in life.

Not that I always followed the straight and narrow. I did take up smoking when I was fifteen. Mom and Dad both smoked, but they did not want us kids to smoke. All the tough guys in the movies smoked, as did most of my friends, so there was some pressure to join the crowd. I'd go into the bathroom when Mom was not home and practice smoking, and cough and cough and cough. I rehearsed holding the cigarette just right, like they did in the movies, and practiced taking a drag without coughing myself to death. I did finally get the hang of smoking and it was probably a couple of years before Mom discovered my habit.

My brother Dick was the opposite of me. I used to think of him as being irresponsible. To some degree he lived up to the reputation my mother gave him. She expected less, so she got less. I recall Dick asking me to watch the store while he went to the bathroom in the back of the house. After about a half hour, I started wondering where he was. I left the store, went through the alley to the back of the house, and looked in the bathroom window. Dick was in there reading a comic book. To me his behavior was a form of irresponsibility. I would never have done that. I thought of it as cheating and being terribly unfair.

Mom would sometimes get after Dick. One day she picked up a shoe with a high heel and went for him, and he grabbed both of her arms. There she was yelling, "You little bastard, you better turn me loose." Dick just said, "No, Mom, I'm not going to, you'll hit me." That was my brother Dick.

Unlike Dick, I had a far greater anxiety about being caught. My fear itself could be an alarming experience for me. One day a young kid who I sometimes liked to hang out with, but who would occasionally bully me, got me upset. Afterward, when I got home, I found his baseball cap there. Thinking I could get even with him, I took the cap out to the road in front of our house and when an old pickup truck came chugging up the hill, I tossed the cap in the bed of the pickup. The driver never noticed and kept going. Now that may not seem like any great revenge, but I remember going into the house and going upstairs to our bedroom and waiting for the police to arrive. I just thought I had done something so terrible, surely someone would call the cops. I don't think my fears all came from my mother. But she did teach me a basic sense of responsibility and fairness.

Then there was the time, during my high school years, when I went to a Saturday matinee movie alone, which was rare for me to do. I was fifteen at the time. There were only about a dozen people in the theater. During the show, an "older" woman, about twenty years old, came in and sat down right next to me. That got me nervous. Next thing I knew, she had her hand on my knee. I jumped up and left the theater and headed home. Her behavior just scared the hell out of me. I don't think I ever told Mom about the experience. To me, at that age, there was nothing predictable about where things were going and I didn't like uncertainty.

Dad played less of a role in my life. He was quiet, more withdrawn, and must have seen his role as mostly providing a paycheck for the family. Nonetheless, he contributed in various other ways. He used to give us kids a little spending money, an allowance, and sometimes compensation for the work we did. When I was about fourteen, he bought Dick and me a Czechoslovakian-made motorcycle. These were small bikes, popular in those days and known as Czech motorcycles. We had to use our own spending money to fill it up with gas, but Dick and I rode that cycle for hours and hours.

A few years later, in about 1947, a customer owed Mom and Dad money and Dad accepted a 1935 Ford as pay-

1953 Brother Dick Harper and Dad (Myrl L. Harper)
"Two of my favorite people."

ment. That old car became Dick's and mine to drive. Though it really wasn't ours, we considered it ours and we could drive our friends around in it. Everyone would throw in a nickel or dime for gas and maybe buy a gallon or two.

Gas was twenty-two cents a gallon then. In that respect, I felt my father was pretty good to us.

If any repair work was ever needed on the old car or on our motorcycle, Dick was the one who was eager to do it. He was much more mechanically inclined than I was. He always wanted to know how things worked. He would take a clock apart to see how all the little gears functioned. He would go outdoors in the snow to help someone fix a tire, just to be close to the car. By the time he was sixteen, he probably had taken apart and put back together two or three motorcycles, fixed them up, and sold them. Later, for years and years, he worked on his own cars. I guess he still does. I think our dad approved of his interests. As for myself, I could admire him for having those skills, but I never wanted any part of the grease and all. I was aiming for the white-collar job.

Our dad was not a sportsman. He didn't hunt or fish and had no time for any kind of athletics. His influence may be one reason for my lack of interest in sports. My youngest brother, Gary, became an avid athlete and played football and basketball. I can remember Dad saying Gary would never amount to anything because all he ever did was bounce a basketball up and down the street. Dad never attended any of Gary's ball games. He just never thought a person should waste their time on sports, or even music, for that matter. Dad was macho but not sports oriented.

One of the things we liked doing with the spending money Dad gave us was to go to the movies. Probably the earliest memory I have is one of going to the movies with my parents, to a drive-in movie theater. I was probably only three years old at the time. Movies continued to be a favorite pastime for me. We'd often go on to the Saturday afternoon matinee. The theater was in the old downtown part of Cumberland and, in the 1940s, going to the movies was the only way we ever got to enjoy air conditioning in the summer time. For me it was always an experience of being transported into another world, with the comfortable coolness and the exciting life portrayed on the screen. Coming out afterward and being hit with the sweltering, late afternoon heat that brought us back to reality was always a letdown.

Mom and Dad generally went to the movies on their own in the evenings, as Mom preferred the romantic stuff. We liked the B-grade cowboy flicks with Roy Rogers, Gene Autry, John Wayne; and the war movies, the action films. We didn't care for romance, not that we had no interest in girls. We just didn't want to see romance in a movie. If a cowboy ever kissed a girl, we probably wouldn't go to the same movie again. That is the way we felt.

The good guys and the bad guys were always clearly defined in the movies we saw, never any shades of gray. Vigilantes were considered to be among the bad guys; you couldn't take the law into your own hands. If any vigilantes showed up, John Wayne or some such figure would always be waiting in the wings to make sure the law was honored in the end.

The war movies, in retrospect, had an interesting twist to them. During World War II, we saw movies about the war on the eastern front with the Russians fighting the Nazis, and films depicting the Americans in Europe and in the Pacific. When I was a youngster, the Russians were the good guys, allies of the Americans, fighting to defeat the tyranny of the Nazis. They were heroic, good-looking, healthy men and women. The German soldiers were always portrayed as being big, ugly people; and the average Japanese had coke-bottle glasses and buckteeth, looking mean as the devil.

The usual unambiguous divide we saw in the movies between the good guys and the bad guys suddenly changed right after World War II ended in 1945. Speculation soon circulated that our next war would probably be with Russia. I was shocked to hear such comments and couldn't understand why we would want to fight these good people who were the heroes in the movies?

My high school years were all spent at Allegany High in Cumberland. The first couple of years were uneventful. If anything, I developed an inferiority complex. It came from the peer pressure and the kids I perceived as being from more well-to-do families. We didn't have really fancy clothes in those days, but I remember in high school, the white shirt was important to me because white shirts were what the rich kids wore to school: just a regular dress shirt, a white shirt with long sleeves; no tie or coat. Some of my friends lived on Washington Street in Cumberland, the more upscale neighborhood, and they all wore white shirts. Wearing a white shirt became, for me, a sign I was on par with them. I remember it took a bit of persuading before my mother got the picture that I needed to fit in and I was becoming status conscious.

Not that I applied myself harder to my schoolwork. I must not have made a clear connection between education and status acquisition. Projecting myself as being successful, combined with a willingness to work harder than others, was what I felt guaranteed success. For some reason my understanding didn't include schoolwork. I still mostly got C grades and had to struggle to get a B and really work hard to get an A. I could never accept a D or F, though I may have gotten one occasionally. I could accept a C because I felt I was average when it came to academics and other things associated with school. Maybe I was and that is why I recognized my ambitions would have to find another road to success.

My attitude began to change some in 1948, during my junior year of high school. I registered for a typing class because I felt typing skills might someday be required of me if

I was going to have a white-collar job, although typing was usually done by female secretaries at the time; and in a class of twenty-five there were only five boys. At that point I had no thoughts about going to college. I concluded I would graduate from high school and get some sort of office job. I had no desire to be a coal miner, railroader, or laborer of any kind. I just envisioned myself as one day wearing a white shirt and tie and thought typing would get me closer to my goal.

The typing teacher was Mrs. Claire Livesey, a rather short, maybe five feet two, woman who was a touch on the plump side. A Southerner, from Kentucky, she had dark hair and wore glasses. She was not excessively proper but proper, nonetheless. I remember she could not pronounce the letter F; it always came out "alf," or something like that. Otherwise, there was nothing particularly striking about her. She was kind of a strict teacher, not really warm and friendly. Half the students liked her and the other half just tolerated her.

For some reason, and I have never understood why, Mrs. Livesey took a special interest in helping me develop socially and emotionally. Something caused her to encourage me—and it was not because I was a "teacher's pet." I did not bring her apples or candy or anything. I guess she saw this young introvert who she felt was more capable and she wanted to help me. I ended up taking two years of typing with her.

As a result of her encouragement, there were extracurricular activities I got involved in that I otherwise would not have on my own. I joined the glee club and the school choir. I remember being in a few stage plays because she pushed me to try out for roles. I helped put the school yearbook together my senior year. Before, not being an athlete had left me feeling introverted and inferior. I had felt like I was not capable of doing things "real" boys did, and I had no desire to even try.

Mrs. Livesey taught me through the encouragement she gave me to recognize other kinds of activities that could be equally meaningful. She saw something in me I did not see. She demon-strated a confidence in me that I did not have in myself. She influenced me to ask questions about myself, drew me out of myself, and gave me social skills that served me well later on.

Looking back, I feel she was one of the more significant influences of my development during my adolescent years. She really didn't have to take a special interest in me; but, I

"I was voted 'most handsome boy' in my senior class. Honest!"

1950 Ron Harper High school Graduation - 17 years old

suppose, helping students catch sight of their real potential is what keeps many teachers inspired. For me, her concern made a big difference. She really was my *second significant role model*, someone to whom I continue to feel indebted for what she taught me about myself.

Perhaps it was because of Mrs. Livesey's influence, and my not having any other options planned, that I began entertaining the idea of going to a teacher's college after graduating from high school. Some of the other kids were going to college and I began seeing it as the route to the white-collar job I ultimately wanted. At the same time, I had no desire to leave home. I knew kids who got jobs in Ohio and other places and just up and moved. I could not imagine, at that point, doing such a thing. I guess I was too much of a momma's boy. Even as a senior in high school, I recall the warm feeling I'd get at the end of the day heading home, knowing Mom would be there. Frostburg State Teachers College, however, was only twelve miles up the road, and I was contemplating commuting to school there.

In the meantime, there was another part of my life where I was learning and developing. I joined the local Cumberland, Maryland, United States Marine Corp Reserve unit when I was just fifteen years old. I joined in 1948, when I was halfway through high school. All the war movies I had been seeing probably had some influence on me wanting to join, but there was a more immediate reason as well. During study hall at school I sat behind a boy who mentioned to me one day that he was in the Marine Reserves. He got me interested and told me about his experience and how much money he was making for going to drill once a month. He told me that he had a uniform and about his marksmanship training and such. He made the reserves sound easy and fun.

I can't say I had much of a patriotic motive for joining. By then I'd learned plenty about world conflicts from the movies I'd seen, but I didn't really keep up with current events. Six years earlier, when the Japanese bombed Pearl Harbor, I had been totally confused. My parents had a friend at the time named Pearl. And when I heard on the radio all the talk about bombing Pearl Harbor, the first thought I had was the Japanese had bombed this woman. I couldn't comprehend why the Japanese would want to bomb a woman, just one person. Well, I had learned a few things since then, but still, joining the reserves for me was about earning money for having fun one day a month. The possibility that the reserves could lead to me finding myself on the frontline of some foreign war just didn't occur to me.

Anyway, I went down and signed up, fudging a bit on my age, telling them I was seventeen. Those signing me up didn't seem concerned that I looked young. After signing up, I got my own uniform and, once a month, I'd ride my bike five miles to get to the place where we trained. The extra spending money I got for my efforts came in handy. When summer rolled around and we were required to spend two weeks down in Camp Lejeune, North Carolina, I didn't mind. The entire unit rode down to the base and back on the train. I may not have been much of an athlete, but this kind of activity suited me well. Before long, I had been promoted from private to private first class to corporal.

I graduated from high school in June of 1950 at the age of seventeen, and the following month my Marine Corp unit was activated. It meant we'd all be going to Camp Lejeune for further training and possible assignment elsewhere. I basically was beginning what ended up being an eighteen-month period of active duty, a time of transition in my life from youth to adulthood. There went my plans for going to teacher's college in the fall. Yet, having been to Camp Lejeune the two summers before and given I'd be going with my unit, I wasn't upset. The North Korean Army had invaded South Korea at the end of June, which is what prompted the call-up of my unit, and many other reserve units. But for me, Korea was some place far away. This development didn't concern me much.

The hot summer evening when we all got on the train to ride down to North Carolina remains a poignant memory, one that continues to make me get teary-eyed every time I think of it. The families of all the young men in my unit came down to the train station to see their loved ones off. Mom and Dad and my two brothers and sister all came along with me. When the train whistle sounded the last call to board, my mom, in her usual manner, was all hugs and kisses. My brothers and sister were, in turn, wishing me well. Then, I turned to my dad to shake his hand—he never hugged us—and, I saw tears in his eyes. My departure became very emotional for me.

Up until that point, I had never felt my father loved me. Yes, I use to think he liked me, but there was little indication he really loved me. He just never went out of his way to do things with us kids. All those extracurricular school activities I'd been a part of, the theater plays I had participated in, the glee club, the choir, my mom used to always come to see me perform, but never my father. He'd always say he had work to do or had something else going on. In that moment, just before I boarded the train, seeing those tears welling up in his eyes made me realize I was loved, not just by my mother, but by my father as well. Minutes later the train was rolling and I was caught up in excited conversations with my buddies. But I never forgot those tears in my father's eyes.

For the most part, the year-and-a-half I spent in the Marines was a wonderful part of my life. I didn't see combat, so I don't have the horrors of war haunting me. Life in the Marines, for me, was more like cowboy games for grown-ups. At age seventeen, I was dressed in a uniform, with a helmet and a real rifle, and spent days on the firing range shooting real bullets. We were like people I had seen in movies, John Wayne on Iwo Jima, that sort of thing.

I spent most of my time in the service at Camp Lejeune, except for a few forays elsewhere during training exercises, including a two-week stint in the Caribbean off the coast of Puerto Rico. Conditions at the time were a bit chaotic because the Pentagon was rapidly deploying troops west to California and on to Korea. Most of the enlisted men who were straight out of high school were being sent to Parris Island for boot camp. Since I had been in the reserves and had some training and was already a corporal, they didn't want to put me, and others in my position, in boot camp with all the new recruits. Instead, they had us take a written test, which I passed, and I was exempted from having to go to boot camp. I was pleased, because I had heard horror stories about boot camp training.

I ended up in a casual company, H Company, Third Battalion, Sixth Regiment, in a staging area. My unit was an infantry unit but we were not assigned to do anything in particular. Mostly, we were supposed to be available to do odd jobs that needed doing.

I should give the Marine Corps more credit for what I learned during my time on active duty. The Corps certainly taught me how to get along with a diverse group of people. The military had been racially integrated for the first time shortly before I was activated. Fifty guys shared a barracks, with bunk beds lining both sides. There were kids from New York and hillbillies from Mississippi and Alabama, kids from small towns, city kids and farm kids. I got along with all of them. Some of the others struggled to get along with people they thought were different from themselves. Two or three of the guys in my barracks were black fellows (called Negroes back then), which upset some of the white guys from the Deep South who didn't think blacks deserved to be in the Marines. But I liked the black guys and respected them for the hard work they did. For me, diversity was not a problem.

The Marine Corps also reinforced my self-confidence and a sense of discipline already there. And I acquired leadership and management skills that would serve me well in the future. I started out as a corporal, which meant I led a team of four, including myself. Later, I became a squad leader with command over eight men. As a young person, still a kid in many respects, the responsibility was good for me.

Not that everything went smoothly, nor did I always toe the line. Early in my time at Camp Lejeune, someone

1952 U.S. Marine Corps,
Sgt. Ronald L. Harper, nineteen years old
"I always liked the Marine Corp dress blue uniform,
but not on me."

came into the barracks one day and said, "Hey, we need a typist. Does anyone here know how to type?" Typing sounded like a good deal to me, something that might get me out of more rigorous assignments. I went down to an office and typed for a day. They kept me until about eight or nine at night. I didn't like having to work late, so the next day I didn't go. Now, one thing you don't do in the

Marines is not show up for assignments. They were so dis-
organized; if they missed me, they didn't know where I
was. They never came after me.

A few days later, someone came in and said, "We have an
opening at the 'slop shute.'" The slop shute was the beer parlor on the base where drinks were served to enlisted men, and
pool tables and other forms of entertainment were available.
I'd been observing the infantry units early in the mornings,
marching with heavy packs on, rifles slung over their shoulders, and I didn't want any part of it. The slop shute sounded
good to me and I volunteered.

I spent the next three months serving beers, mixing milk
shakes, and cleaning tables for infantrymen coming in from
hard days of training. When we weren't busy, I was playing
pool. We had it easy, and my co-workers used to speak deri-
sively of the "grunts" who were out there working all day
long, getting dirty, muddy, and doing some real training—the
men we were serving drinks at the end of the day. I can't say
I always felt proud of what I was doing for my country, serving drinks while others were doing such rigorous training.

But the slop shute was not altogether laid back for me.
My supervisor, Sergeant Robert Lee, was a guy from my reserve unit in Cumberland and for some unknown reason he
went out of his way to make life hell for me. He was mean.
He was trying to be the tough guy, and I was in his sights. He
took to hazing me on a daily basis. His treatment of me was
embarrassing because there were others around. He was showing them how tough he could be. This harassment went on
for quite some time. As a young kid, wanting to lift myself up
by the bootstraps and trying to be a Marine, his obnoxious-
ness was painful. He was one of the few people I have known
in life who I truly did not like.

The anger I felt toward him stayed with me long after I was
discharged from the Marines. One gets used to hearing all kinds

of cursing coming from Marines. But this guy overdid it. I had to keep telling myself I had parents who worked long hours to succeed and a mother and a favorite teacher who thought I was somebody, and confidence in myself that I could succeed. To be dictatorial, like he was, yelling and cussing at me the way he did, was no way to treat anyone and not the way I ever wanted to treat anyone else. Unwittingly, he probably helped motivate me to do well in life, to prove he was wrong in the way he used to run me down. Mostly, I just think it was a bad episode, something I wish I could have avoided.

After about three months of my working in the slop shute, a new colonel took charge of the battalion, an Italian guy. He declared that everyone had to be properly

Sgt. Ron Harper, USMC, 19 years old
"Bright eyed and Gung-Ho."

trained. I was yanked out of the slop shute and thrown into infantry training. That is when I really began to enjoy the Marine Corps, the exercise, and the camaraderie. A trip down to Puerto Rico was only one highlight. We did a mock landing on the island of Vieques.

One thing I did in the Marines that I'm not too proud of is drink more than was good for me. As a young seventeen-year-old, I really hadn't drunk much alcohol before going into the service. Then I found myself being the younger kid trying to live up to the ways of guys a few years older than me. What was available was 3.2 percent beer, but I'd still drink more than I should have. Saturday nights I'd go to the slop shute and drink too much. Even on the weekends when I'd catch a ride home to Cumberland with a bunch of other guys, I'd buy some beers, which an underage kid in uniform could do in those days. On one occasion, I went with a group of guys to Richmond, Virginia, and went out drinking with them at a cheap restaurant. They were drinking something I had never had; I drank right along with them. The next thing I knew, I was lying on the floor in the men's room and someone trying to get in was knocking the door against my head. I must have passed out on the floor in there.

I drank so much in the Marine Corps I wondered if I was an alcoholic, and I wasn't sure I was going to be able to control my drinking when I got out. I also began wondering if I'd be able to get up every morning, go to work, and hold down a job without having the regimentation of the Marines. In the service someone told me to get out of bed, and I didn't have a choice. They told me what time to get up, what time to eat breakfast, lunch, dinner, what time to turn the lights out, and so forth. With the freedom I'd have on the outside, I wondered if I would be able to stay disciplined if I continued to drink. I just wasn't sure I could handle life without the regulation. I had this fear: "My God, when I leave the service I'm going to have to go to work every day for the rest of my life, like my dad."

Fortunately, my fears quickly faded after I was discharged from the Marines in January of 1952. I quickly fell in love with what people call "work." And, for the first year after getting out and getting married, I didn't drink anything and didn't want to associate with anyone who did. Much of the credit has to go to someone I met while I was still in the Marines.

1951 Katherine Harper, High School Graduation
"My first real love, and still is."

CHAPTER TWO

Marriage, Early Employment, and Family Life

While I was in the Marine Corps at Camp Lejeune, there was this big fellow in my unit named Alfred Hodges. We were part of a fire team together. I was the corporal in charge of the four-man team and he was under my command as a private first class. On one occasion, he did me a favor that dramatically shaped the rest of my life. Private First Class Hodges introduced me to his sister.

On some weekends, if I had the money, I and four or five other guys would pile in a car and make the ten-hour trip to Cumberland on Friday night and return on Sunday. One weekend, I knew I couldn't afford to go, and Alfred told me his sister was coming to visit him in Wilmington, probably a twenty-five minute bus ride from Camp Lejeune. She was coming down from Charlotte for the weekend. Alfred asked if I would mind dating her. Being his boss, so to speak, as corporal, I thought it was an unusual request. He showed me a picture of her taken with a little Brownie camera, showing her standing beside a street sign in Charlotte. I became more interested. With nothing better to do, I said I would be willing to meet his sister.

We took the bus to Wilmington on Saturday and made our way to where Alfred's wife was staying in an apartment. His wife prepared dinner for us, and then we went to meet his sister, Katherine, at the bus station. I was immediately impressed. This was August 3, 1951. We went to a movie that night, and I put my arm around her, which was kind of a forward thing for me to do. Afterward, we took a walk then sat on the front step of the guesthouse where she was staying and talked and talked until 1:30 in the morning. She claims she knew within an hour after she met me that she was going to marry me.

I had to get back to the base before morning, but she asked if I was coming back the next day. For some reason, I never gave her a straight answer, and she didn't know what to expect. She likes to say my response was that if some guy washed my skivvies (underwear) as he had promised, I'd be back. It may indeed be the answer I gave her. Anyhow, I did return the next day and spent the day and evening with her. Following that visit, we began writing one another and within a short period of time we were discussing marriage.

Right from the beginning, I was very comfortable with Katherine. I respected her and was proud of her. She was also very attractive. Still, I was a bit hesitant at first. I knew committing to her was the right thing to do; I just didn't want to rush into marriage. In her mind, there was no question, because marriages were made in heaven. When she decided an hour after we met that we were going to be married, she felt God caused our relationship to be. Well, I'm not sure God creates those kinds of circumstances. I have never been as certain as she was. (Although after fifty-two years, I think she just might have been right.)

If I had known on my first date with Katherine that she smoked—in those days she smoked two or three cigarettes *a week*—I probably would not have dated her a second time. It was okay for a man to smoke, for me to smoke, but not a woman. But I didn't find out about Katherine's smoking until later and by then, we were truly in love, both of us.

A few weeks after we first met, I was introduced to Katherine's father. Though Katherine and her mother were living in Charlotte, he had recently moved down to Jacksonville, North Carolina, just outside of Camp Lejeune, to take a job as a chef in a restaurant. Her father, kind of a ladies' man himself, never liked any of her boyfriends, and she felt unsure about whether he'd have anything good to say about me afterward. I was in uniform the first time we met, and surprisingly, he liked me, which certainly amazed Katherine.

I don't remember a specific time when I made a decision and then made a marriage proposal to Katherine. I think our relationship kind of evolved until we decided mutually that we were going to get married. Katherine will disagree with me on that point. She swears I proposed, and I must admit, when it comes to details, she has a better memory than I do. But I still claim it was mutual.

I didn't have enough money and couldn't afford to buy her an engagement ring. On the weekends, I could barely come up with enough money to buy a bus ticket to Charlotte to visit her. She was working as a bank teller at the Bank of Charlotte, on Tryon Street, and boasted to me in a letter that she had just gotten a raise from one hundred sixty-five dollars to one hundred eighty dollars *a month*. She took her own savings and bought herself an engagement ring and told me nobody would know the difference. Only after we were married did I buy her another engagement ring to go with the wedding ring I gave her.

I visited with Katherine's father again a few months later and, after a lengthy conversation in which he seemed impressed with me, I asked whether I could borrow his car over the Christmas break. I told him I would like to take Katherine with me to Maryland and introduce her to my parents. He agreed, and I arranged to pick Katherine up in Charlotte the following weekend. Her mother had agreed to the idea earlier, but when I arrived she suddenly changed her mind. She said it probably wasn't a good idea for the two of us to be alone in a car for eleven or twelve hours. Katherine and I were really shook up by her change of view, but Katherine's mother kept insisting, "I'm sure your father won't approve." Katherine went to the phone and called her dad, and her mother got on the phone with him, and Katherine's mother reluctantly agreed to let us go. Her mother needn't have worried. We picked up a soldier on the way and he spent most of the trip sleeping on Katherine's shoulder. She was in the middle and couldn't get out of it.

My folks liked Katherine from the moment they met her. She was a real Southern lady to them. What my folks knew about Southerners was what they had seen in the movies or heard about in school. In their minds the South lost the war, and in the South most people lived in poverty except on the occasional plantation where the filthy rich lived. They figured their son probably wouldn't marry someone in poverty, so she must come from a wealthy family. They envisioned this wealthy young woman who they expected to meet when we got to Cumberland. The subject of her background came up during one conversation when we were asked whether Katherine's home had white pillars on the front. Well, it did. They were about six inches in diameter, enough to support the front porch. My folks imagined a huge plantation mansion with large white columns on the front.

Katherine proved to be even more warmhearted than my mother. She was a very mature young lady. She always had a beautiful smile and was kind and friendly, having a European (Greek, German, Hungarian ancestry) warmth that her family displayed with easy hugs. My folks were not accustomed to all the affection, but they fell in love with her because of it.

When we were leaving to return to North Carolina, my mom and dad felt like they had to give us a gift, but instead of coming up with a present, they gave each of us a ten-dollar bill—a lot of money in those days. They seemed to feel like they had to impress Katherine and they asked me beforehand if ten dollars would be enough.

We had first met in August and by early October we were planning to get married. The only thing holding us back was our waiting for my discharge from the Marines. My getting out was scheduled for early December but then

1951 Our first photo together
"Very much in love. Kat was 17 and I was 18."

was delayed for some reason until January 31, 1952. Our wedding was on February 12.

We were married in St. Patrick's Church in Charlotte, now St. Patrick's Cathedral. I don't remember too many details of that day, other than there being a mix-up and Katherine's family all showed up at the church and forgot to bring her along. She had been dressing, or something, and had to telephone the church for a ride.

My mother and my aunt, Lena Owens, mom's older sister, came down from Maryland by train to attend. Not surprisingly, my father didn't make the trip. He wasn't much into socializing or attending wedding celebrations. I'm not sure he even had a suitable coat and tie for such an occasion.

Our honeymoon consisted of two nights in a room which Katherine's father paid for, in the old Charlotte Hotel on West Trade Street. I don't know if it was planned that way, but the room had twin beds. The wedding party sneaked in before we arrived and filled in between the sheets with cracker crumbs and strung toilet paper all around the room. The next morning at seven, Katherine's brother Alfred called to tell us he and his wife, Janet, were going to join us for breakfast at the hotel. Soon after, Kat's mother called to invite us to an early dinner and a send-off for my mother and Aunt Lena, who were heading back to Maryland that evening on the train. We did get a second night in the hotel, before catching the train ourselves for our move to Cumberland, with tickets paid for with thirty-five dollars Katherine's uncle, Bill Hodges, had given us as a wedding present.

So our honeymoon was kind of short and sweet and we barely got around to trying to figure out what neither of us knew much about. What I knew about sex was mostly from what little my mother had hinted about while teaching me morality and what my boyhood friends had told me, mostly fictitious claims about their sexual conquests. My education didn't get much further when I was serving in the Marines. On our honeymoon, we were just two virgins trying to solve the puzzle for ourselves. We were both so naïve it was pathetic. Later, we had to buy some sex books to find out what making love was all about. *Playboy* used to publish one called *The Forum*, a monthly booklet. We found it to be more realistic and we used to sit and study it together.

One thing I can say is that Katherine and I have been friends from the beginning, and friendship sustained our relationship through some difficult times early in our married life. We started with very little other than the bond of love between us. We more or less accepted the differences between our two families. There were certainly no conflicting cultural differences in the two of us other than the fact that she was Catholic and I had no strong ties to any church. I knew she had graduated from a Catholic school, but religion didn't play a big part in our decision to get married one way or the other. She was not concerned that I was not Catholic and I didn't attend church every Sunday, and she didn't pressure me after marrying to attend Sunday Mass.

I really was a hometown boy and it was my understanding we would get married in Charlotte then move to Cumberland to live and work. Katherine accepted my view without any complaints. When we arrived in Cumberland, my mom was going to let us borrow the family car to go on a more extended honeymoon before settling in, but my brother wrecked the car the week before and that plan was cancelled. We moved in with Mom and Dad, sleeping on the living room pull-out couch that made into a double bed, with a crack down the middle. Everyone else in the family slept upstairs and had to pass through the living room to get to the stairs. Here we were, trying to begin married life, and there was all this traffic through our "bedroom," with my two brothers, my sister, and my parents traipsing through in the middle of the night to go to the bathroom and what not.

I didn't take into consideration when planning our move to Cumberland that the unemployment rate there at the time was terribly high. Dad had continued working for the railroad and he said he would try to get me a job there, but I wasn't interested. I didn't want to be a "dirty railroader."

Not being interested in railroading, I had to look elsewhere for a job. A friend of my father's owned a used car lot and he hired me at twenty-five dollars a week to sweep snow off of cars every morning and do whatever else was needed around the place. The twenty-five dollars was more than I deserved for the little bit I did. A few weeks later, my brother Dick got me a job where he was working in a bakery, and I quit the car lot job to start working there.

A week after I settled into the job at the bakery, Katherine and I rented our own apartment, upstairs over a couple's home, with a separate entrance. The location was a bit depressing, right near the railway track and about four miles from my parents. But we had our own little kitchen, bedroom, and bathroom, in short, our own privacy—a place to ourselves.

Katherine found a job in the bookkeeping department at the local Montgomery Ward department store. She did well. My new job at the bakery, before long, began seeming very robotic to me. A conveyer belt brought little strips of dough down toward me and two other men who stood opposite me. They would take the strips of dough and somehow twist them around one another so they became one and put them in pans that had three slots in them. I would grab the pans and put them on a rack behind me. That is all I did at the bakery. The conveyor belt never stopped. The two guys never stopped. If I had to go to the restroom, I had to wait for somebody to replace me because the dough kept coming. The job was not very exciting, and I began thinking it was not a position that took advantage of my two years of typing skills, my experience in the Marine Corps, and all my other aptitudes.

If I were going to advance, it would have been to the job my brother Dick had. He worked the ovens, an unbearably hot job, standing in front of the ovens and throwing pans of dough in, then removing them after the dough had baked. We all wore white T-shirts, but it wasn't the white shirt kind of job I wanted, especially the way our T-shirts used to get filthy with grease. I think of working in the bakery as my first real job, paying union wages of forty-two dollars a week, which covered the rent and gave Katherine and I our independence. Yet, I basically hated that job, and after about three months of it, I concluded my future did not lie in the bakery business.

By then word had filtered down to Katherine's parents in Charlotte that I was not happy with my job. Wanting very much to see us living in North Carolina, Katherine's father began hunting around for a job that might entice me. He lined up a position driving a bakery truck for Mother's Bread for sixty-five dollars a week and told me I would be going to work at about nine or ten in the morning and getting off at about two or three in the afternoon. The type of work sounded appealing to me and I agreed to take the job.

In retrospect, I am a bit surprised I agreed so readily to move. I really didn't want to be far from home, from my mother. Not that she tried to get me to stay in Cumberland. She had seen Charlotte when she went down for our wedding. In those days, Charlotte was much smaller, a clean, beautiful, and friendly city. I think both Mom and Dad thought I might have a better chance in life and work if we moved to Charlotte.

At the same time, the truth about Cumberland was becoming more apparent to me. Cumberland got stuck in the 1930s, the Depression era, and had never gotten out. I couldn't see much future there. Moving to Charlotte made all the sense in the world. We got on a train and moved to Charlotte, in June 1952. We didn't have anything to bring with us except a few clothes.

We moved in with Katherine's parents when we arrived. Her father had returned from Jacksonville and opened his own restaurant in Charlotte. We paid them ten dollars a week for

1952 With Father-in-law, Jimmy Hodges
(Mr. Hodges Greek name is Demetri Hadgopoulos)
"My first taste of wine."

"room and board," which even in those days was cheap. The food we ate cost more than that.

Still, we had difficulty saving money. We just blew it. We were young and in love and enjoyed going to the movies and buying hotdogs and such activities. But once we decided to get our own apartment, it was amazing how much we were willing to start counting the pennies. We found a little place

66

on Wilmar Street. The apartment was so small we had to pass through the bathroom to get to the bedroom. Katherine's father couldn't understand why we would move from a home the size of his to this little, dinky apartment. For me, the experience was an important lesson in life. The dwelling, no matter how humble, *was ours*; we were paying the rent on it. To this day, we have fond memories of the time we shared in that little place.

The job with Mother's Bread that had enticed me to move to Charlotte turned out to entail more work than I had been told. I was trained not so much to drive a truck but to run a bread route. I'd go to work at about five in the morning and

1953 Ron Harper's 20th Birthday, with Katherine's Father and Mother,
Jimmy and Margaret Hodges
"A special occassion."

get home at six or seven at night. Driving the same route every day in a large, boxy bread truck, I delivered bread, sweet rolls, and oatmeal cookies to grocery stores and supermarkets. Some of the more interesting places I went to were in black neighborhoods out in the Beatties Ford Road area. One place I remember was called The Red Front Grocery, painted all red. They were some of the friendliest customers I had and they used to buy a lot of sweet rolls and bread.

Following the same routine every day did get boring, however, and not everything went smoothly. The managers at Winn Dixie would count and inspect everything I delivered, which I didn't like, though I understand better now. It was not unusual for me to go into a grocery store or supermarket and find that the bread I had put in the day before had been squeezed and put toward the back by competing bread deliverers. Sometimes I'd help myself to oatmeal cookies as I was driving the route. An inventory would always be taken at the end of the day and any shortages would be docked from my pay. I also began realizing most of the other workers in the company were no more than ten years older than me. With those guys having more seniority than me, it would be years before I got off that truck and moved into any kind of supervisor's position in the company. Driving a bread truck just wasn't the dream job I was looking for.

Another opportunity arose after I'd been doing the bread route for only three months. Katherine's brother Alfred had been discharged from the Marines and at that time was working for a company called Charlotte Textile Engravers, located on Elizabeth Avenue in Charlotte. He was offered a promotion but couldn't accept the new position until a replacement was found for his old position. He asked me if I'd be interested in what was really just a common laborer's job. Though it was not the white-collar job I wanted, my decision to go for the interview proved to be a good move. This was the job where I first got started working in the production of rollers for printing presses, beginning at the bottom of the ladder.

The owner of the company, a gentleman named Al Scala, interviewed me for the job. He was an Italian fellow, nice-looking, balding, with a wonderful smile. Like a real politician, he seemed to know how to always say the right thing. He offered to pay me seventy-five cents an hour if I took the job, which was the legal minimum wage. Feeling confident, I insisted on eighty cents an hour and he agreed. I went home and told Katherine I was going to begin working at *above* minimum wage.

Charlotte Textile Engravers (later renamed ABC Industries) employed forty to fifty people when I started. I stayed with the company for about nine years, moving up into supervision/management and eventually becoming vice president and assistant Southern district general manager. But I began at the bottom.

In my first position, I did little more than transfer from one room to another rollers that were being prepared for printing fabrics in textile mills. Starting with copper cylinders about five inches in diameter and forty to sixty inches long, I'd insert steel shafts in them and fasten the cylinders onto the shafts. These rollers then had to be transferred from one operation to the next in the process of etching an image onto the roller.

In what was called the copy room a Latvian fellow, Janis Helmanis, who I got along well with, worked the copy machine, which would transfer images to be printed from photographic negatives onto the rollers. Janis would help me lift the rollers into the copy machine and then set up the negatives, which were wrapped around the specially coated cylinders and then exposed to a bright light. These negatives would have an image made up of little dots, like what is used for the photos one sees in newspapers. The copper cylinders had a coating on them that would harden where light penetrated through the negative, between the dots. Once the image transfer was completed, we'd load the rollers back onto the little carts built with special slings for holding them and I'd move them into the next room where the etching took place.

When I first went to work at Charlotte Textile Engravers, Al Scala, the company owner, personally worked in the etching room. There the rollers had to be lifted into a position where they could be dipped into a tank containing an acid. When the cylinder was immersed and rotated in the acid, the acid would eat away the areas on the cylinder coating that were still soft, making little dimple holes called cells that would eventually carry the viscous dyes the printer used. The design that first came off the negative was acid etched into the surface of the cylinder.

The etching process didn't just happen automatically. The person in charge had to dip the cylinder then rinse it off with water and examine it with a magnifying glass to check on the progress of the acidic process. This job took a good eye to see the details and an awareness of what was considered optimum in order to decide if more dipping was needed. Typically, a cylinder was repeatedly dipped and examined before the desired results were achieved. The technology has changed considerably since then, but that is how it was when I started. Draperies, dress goods, and other kinds of printed fabrics were printed with roller plates produced with this method.

It wasn't long before Mr. Scala began noticing I had an aptitude for more than just moving rollers around from room to room. I took an interest in the whole process and was eager to learn. He liked my eagerness and started teaching me to do the etching, letting me use the magnifying glass and instructing me how to judge precise widths of the microscopic cells being etched into the cylinders and to recognize optimum widths of the walls between the cells. With a little training, I got good at it, and Mr. Scala turned over to me the job he had been doing himself.

At home I could count on plenty of encouragement and support from Katherine, who by then was obviously pregnant. Even though I was working steadily, we weren't sure how we were going to pay for our first baby. We just didn't have the money for the hospital and doctor bills and such. Then, along about October, a few months before the baby was born, I unexpectedly received a check for three hundred dollars from the U.S. Marine Corps. A note informed me the check was back pay for my "overseas duty," that was the brief training stint I'd done in the Caribbean. It is hard to imagine three hundred dollars would have paid the whole bill, but as I recall, it did.

The due date for our first baby was December 1952, ten months after we were married. And in 1952 people used to count on their fingers to make sure nine months had passed after marriage before the birth of the first baby. Premarital sex was, to put it lightly, frowned on. Sadly, however, the little boy was stillborn, choked by the umbilical cord wrapped around his neck. The loss was very difficult for both of us. We had planned to name him Ronald Lee Harper Jr. Katherine actually never saw the baby. I went to the funeral home and photographed him in the casket so she would at least have a picture. The priest who visited us said the death was a terrible tragedy but assured us we could have more children. The weeks following were a tough time for us. We managed to move on, and before long Katherine was pregnant again. During the following nine years we had five more children, all of whom we love dearly:

Our Children

Name	Nickname	Born
Daniel Howard	Danny	1953
Ronald James	Jim	1955
Margaret Marie	Margie	1956
Christopher Wayne	Chris	1958
Georgia Kay	Georgia	1961

1954 Dad (Myrl Harper) and our oldest son, Danny Harper
"One of my most favorite photos."

My new job continued to preoccupy me much of the time, with an increasing amount of personal mentoring coming from Mr. Scala. He must have seen something about me that I had not seen myself. He had a son attending college who was only a year younger than me and he probably thought of me as being like another son. Anyway, he took a special interest in training me, first to take over the etching process, then assigning me other responsibilities. While doing so he instilled even more confidence in me. Before long, I was teaching someone else to do the etching and I moved on to supervising half-a-dozen men who had various tasks assigned to them in the production process.

Toward the end of my first year of working at Charlotte Textile Engravers, Katherine and I planned a well-earned vacation trip to Maryland to visit my family. As I was leaving work just before we were going to depart, Mr. Scala brought an envelope by and said to me, "Don't open this until you get home." When I got home and opened the envelope, there was

1955 Our first home, on Lyndhurst Avenue, Charlotte, NC
"We were so proud. It was ours! We paid $4,800."

a twenty-dollar bill inside. Twenty dollars was a heck of a lot of money back in those days. There was also a little note saying, "Ronnie, take good care of your eyes." He had taught me to do the delicate task of inspecting the etchings on the printer cylinders, a job that took good eyesight. It occurred to me he

1954 Al Scala, my mentor and boss
*"One of the four people who had a substantially
positive influence on my life."*

was also saying between the lines, "If your parents in Maryland start twisting your arm to move back, remember you have a good job here in Charlotte, and you have people who want you here and are supportive." The twenty-dollar bill was probably more important to me than the note. Today, the memory of that note is most important, even though the twenty dollars went a long way.

Mr. Scala continued to mentor me and add to my responsibilities in various ways. I had a tremendous respect for the guy. He was always the first one at the office and the last one to leave. I learned from his example. More and more, I began to travel with him to the textile mills to visit our customers. Mr. Scala was an articulate individual and good salesman. I would watch and listen to the way he made his sales pitches, then note how he would follow up with our customers. He not only remembered people's names but also would know the names of men's wives and children and would ask how they were doing. He always put in long hours. My admiration for him kept growing.

Mr. Scala taught me to run up stairs. His office was on the second floor of the plant and he always would run up the steps to get there. When going through the plant, he walked at a fast pace. If I were accompanying him, I'd keep right up with him. I wanted to be like him. He approached his work with a sense of urgency. The importance of being in a hurry in life, being in a hurry to get things done, is something I learned from Al Scala. Perhaps hurrying left me, over the long run, never satisfied with what I have accomplished, but it was one of those values Mr. Scala ingrained in me. Next to my mother, my high school typing teacher, and my wife, he really was another one of my *most significant role models.*

The extra attention he gave me and the way he started pushing me up the ladder created resentment among some of the other employees. Here was this kid, Ronnie Harper, being moved up to positions of responsibility over other people. I have always tried not to generate that sort of bitterness. My personality is one that seeks to avoid confrontation. But envy is a fact of life, quite natural, and something I had to learn to live with. First, I took over the job the owner of the company had been doing. Next, I was moved into a position as a supervisor. Eventually, I became the assistant manager, then the plant manager, and,

1953 Katherine with our third car, a pre-owned 1949 Buick
"Movin' on up."

1956 Our next pride and joy
"Wow! Our first brand new Dodge, and we could almost afford the payments."

at age twenty-four, the general manager of a new plant in Greenville, South Carolina, with the title of vice president and assistant Southern district manager. Some of the old-timers had a problem with the way things were headed.

Mr. Scala must have had a lot of confidence in me. When he decided to expand and open the manufacturing

76

plant in Greenville, he selected me to take charge of the new operation. We leased an old building and assembled equipment to basically do what we did in Charlotte. Although my title was assistant Southern district manager, in a small company a manager wears several hats. As a young, totally inexperienced manager, I did the hiring and staffed the facility. I supervised about fifteen people, physically doing some of the work while training others to do it, including the etching. In addition, I was the entire sales force, taking over much of the South Carolina and Georgia district. I must add, at the beginning, my new position was not a good experience for me, being far away from Charlotte, being so inexperienced and naïve.

I began to make up for my lack of a higher education by reading everything I could get my hands on having to do with business. Mr. Scala saw to it that I had opportunities to attend training seminars. Once he paid all my expenses and let Katherine and me stay in his home in New Jersey during a two-week period in which I attended an American Management Association training seminar in New York City. Later he paid for me to attend the Dale Carnegie course, something I found most helpful and rewarding. And there were many other courses.

Katherine attended my graduation ceremony from the Dale Carnegie course and was inspired to take the seminar herself. As I recall, the seminar was not cheap, and she was only working part time as a bank teller in Greenville at the time. I suggested she ask her boss at work to cover the cost of the training, which he did, for Katherine and two or three other employees. That helped put us on the same wave length regarding our attitudes toward work.

There was a side to taking these seminars that was always tough for me. On the opening day of a seminar, I always had to face an uncomfortable question from the other participants. The first question that always came up was, "Where did you go to school?" I knew they were not asking where I went to high school, and I was left feeling inferior, knowing I had not attended college. Experiences like those were big motivators for me. Over the years I've been an avid reader, mostly regarding business and technical developments. I think I've learned more than a college education would have taught me, and I've had to learn in practical, on-the-job ways.

Some of that education came at a fast and furious pace. In my years of managing the plant in Greenville, between 1957 and 1960, I spent about half my time traveling. I drove a huge, new Oldsmobile station wagon, our personal car, and would visit a half-dozen textile mills in my district to try to drum up business contracts. I'd meet with plant managers and print managers, and sometimes their customers, namely textile designers who would fly in from New York. In those days I felt my inexperience and worried people wouldn't take me seriously. I didn't have any gray hair and all my customers were much older and more knowledgeable than I was. The pressure made me work harder, trying to prove myself

I was mostly selling engraving services. If a customer wanted, for example, to print a flag on a piece of fabric or drapery, the customer would give me a design on paper, where an artist had painted the flag, and the customer would say, "This is what I want you to do." We would engrave two cylinders. One cylinder for the blue on the flag and another cylinder showing all the red. Then, in the printing process on white cloth, the two cylinders would be synchronized so the images met at the right place.

Keeping new business coming in was always a challenge. The backlog of orders was either feast or famine. One week the employees would be sitting around with too little to do; and the following week they might have more than they could handle. As the salesperson, I was under constant pressure.

We only had one competitor, Consolidated Engravers, also based in Charlotte, but they were enough to create a cutthroat selling environment. Whoever had the lowest price typically got the job. Or, if we could deliver in two weeks and the Consolidated was going to take four, we would get the job. There was very little customer loyalty.

While I was preoccupied with my responsibilities, keeping up with demands at work, at home Katherine kept busy caring for our growing family. When we moved to Greenville

Left to right: Kat's mother, Margaret; 1st son, Danny; Ron's mother, Dolly; 2nd son, Jimmy; Ron's Aunt Nelly; Kat's father, Jimmy; Kat's Aunt Edna
"Heading toward five children. Note, two in this picture."

in 1957, we already had three children: Danny, Jimmy, and Margie. Chris and Georgia were born in Greenville.

More than I really care to admit, I was probably much like my father when it came to not participating a whole

1961 Ron holding Georgia
"Our baby daughter."

lot in helping to raise our kids when they were young. I felt it was a woman's job and went along with what Katherine said. I took children to be just a natural part of a marriage and don't know if I ever got visibly excited about the birth of a baby. In retrospect, I won't say I'm proud of my approach. I was, however, always happy for Katherine, because a birth for her was just a wonderful, wonderful event, a very happy time in her life. Being pregnant for most of the first nine years of our marriage, including our first baby, who we lost at birth, and raising our five surviving children was a heroic effort on her part.

I do have regrets about not spending more time with Katherine and the family when I was younger. My work consumed most of my time and energy. I don't know how she put up with my hours when she had five kids at home. During some periods, there were two in diapers. When I see young women with one baby consuming all their time, I just can't imagine how Katherine coped with five kids, mostly on her own. But she did. Later, after our kids were in school, Katherine generally worked part time. She

1962 Margie, Christopher, Katherine and, Jimmy Harper
"Easter Sunday, dress-up time."

81

worked for a while at Sears, then at Kmart. Later, she went to work at Wachovia Bank, all the while making sure our children were well cared for.

As a grandfather, I think I am more attentive to my grandchildren than I was to my own children. I'll watch a grandchild just learning to walk or do something else new for the

1962 Katherine and Ron
"In Miami, I think."

first time and say to Katherine, "Wow, look what she is doing." And Katherine will say, "Yes, our own children were the same way at that stage. You were just never home to see them growing up."

Katherine was the one who made sure the kids had their books and clothes ready for school, had breakfast before they went to school, and got out the door on time. She enrolled them in the Catholic school to begin with. Later she pulled them out of the Catholic school and put them in a public school because the Catholic school was so small she didn't think they would get a good education there.

She was more apt to take them to the doctor if they needed it. The worst mishaps requiring a doctor were, first, when Jimmy fell through bleachers at a ball game and blood was gushing out of his head. And, second, when our son Chris, at about ten years old, just about burned himself up. He and a friend were playing with a model airplane and they thought it would be fun to douse it with gasoline and watch it burn. Then Chris's friend decided to put a little more gasoline on the fire, which caused an explosion. In a panic, he threw the gas can, which hit Chris, and the flames

1963 Katherine
"My lovely wife."

jumped to Chris's chest. Chris ended up hospitalized for several days with burns all over.

We faced the usual sorts of problems parents have raising kids and my response was probably not atypical from a lot of dads. I think until they were out of their teens, my kids probably feared me as much as I used to fear my father. Not because I disciplined them much, which I didn't enjoy doing, but because I just was not involved with them on a daily basis. I was too busy with work and justified my lifestyle by telling myself I had to make a living and provide for them.

I did participate as a weekend dad sometimes. With Katherine taking the initiative, we used to enjoy Sunday afternoon outings and picnics. These events were pretty important to us. And we did take vacations together as a family. It wasn't like I wanted to stay away from the kids and never wanted anything to do with them.

Unlike my own father, I did encourage my kids to get involved in extracurricular activities at school. Danny and Chris both played football and I occasionally went to watch their games. There were a few Parent-Teacher Association meetings I went to, which is more than my father did. I probably consciously realized Dad hadn't spent much time with me and I would have to do a better job with my children. But I really didn't do much more than he did.

As a father, I think I did a lot of compromising. I wasn't a dictatorial father who said you do it my way or else. I respected my kids' feelings. Though I didn't always appreciate what they were doing or agree with them, I tried to understand them. Like when Danny, a bit of a rebel as a kid, came home one day with a huge German shepherd dog. I was scared half to death of the animal and insisted he get a fence and keep it on the back porch. Danny soon lost interest in cleaning up after it and I would have to go out and hose the porch down to get rid of the crap all over the concrete. The day that dog jumped up on me and knocked me down was a day I had to summon up a lot of understanding.

There was the time we bought a used motor scooter for Danny, thinking he would enjoy it. Before we realized what was happening, he had taken the thing completely apart and wasn't able to get it back together. He did things like that. We never figured out why he took the scooter apart in the first place.

Our children grew up in the 1960s. Appreciate the fact that I grew up in an era when men kept their hair short, so they looked like they were in the military whether they were or not. And I had been in the Marines and kept my hair short after I got out. Well, none of our kids became flower children or anything of the kind, but at one point, our son Jimmy let his hair grow down to where it touched his ears. Long hair was kind of the in thing for the kids at school during those days. After all, the Beatles wore theirs down over their ears, and the kids were letting their hair grow a little longer. But it really aggravated the devil out of me. I was the one who cut the kids' hair and I was just going to cut it off his ears. I just didn't want his hair touching his ears. He was about fifteen, and when I sat him down for a haircut, he just started crying. Finally, I relented and decided long hair was more important to him than short hair was to me, so I didn't cut it.

A year or two later, my hair was growing down over my ears because that was the in look. There are pictures of me with hair over my ears and with long sideburns. The seventies look is what it was. My hair was so long that when I was flying—and in those days they didn't have the ramp to the airplane, you had to go out to the tarmac—on a windy day my hair was all over the place. I got to the point where I was using hair spray on it, like Katherine did. My father would have thought hair spray was really silly, because Dad use to put Rose Tonic or hair oil on his hair to keep it slicked down.

You could tell anytime that an average male sat back in a chair, because there was a grease spot. Times do change.

Katherine had been raised with a father who worked long hours and contributed little to life around the home. Even after I got to know her father, he used to go to work at his restaurant, the Lafayette Grill, on Morehead Street in Charlotte, at 5:00 a.m. and stay busy until 9:00 p.m., though sometimes he'd take off an hour or two in the afternoon before the dinner customers started coming in. He stood on his feet all day doing most of the cooking and would come home with swollen ankles. For me, he was one more example of what a man needed to do to succeed. Katherine seemed to accept her father's work habits, to think of them as normal. She never questioned my work schedule. She had watched her father work long hours all her life.

To my knowledge, the notion of a "workaholic" did not exist back in those days. Memories of the Depression were still fresh in most people's minds and anyone who had a job was grateful. I also realize that for people like me, there never was much of a disjuncture between work life and private life. I was not the kind of person who would watch the clock at the end of the day and just want to get home, or would say, "Thank goodness it's Friday" and look forward to the weekend. Beginning with my job with Charlotte Textile Engravers, I *never did work for a living;* I lived to work, and loved the challenges. I used to be up early in the morning and out on the job, and would bring a briefcase home at seven or eight at night, have dinner, and open the briefcase to continue my assignments. I would have a hot cup of coffee in front of me from the time I got up until the time I went to bed and the caffeine would keep me in high gear. I really don't know how Katherine put up with me for all those years. I don't think it was for the money; she tolerated my habits and ambitions because she saw me progressing. I have to marvel at her for having done so.

There were financial rewards for my work efforts. When I first started working, in 1952, my goal had been to earn a dollar an hour. After I achieved that goal, I starting thinking of ten thousand dollars a year as a goal. In 1960, my last year of managing the Greenville plant, I succeeded. That level of income put us in a standard of living of young, upper-middle-income family. When we first moved to Greenville, we paid twelve thousand five hundred dollars for a new, twelve-hundred-square-foot home. This price may not sound like much now, just like the house seems small for a family with five kids. But we were above average. This was the fifties, when Dwight D. Eisenhower was president. A new home, on average, cost twenty-two thousand dollars. A new car cost one thousand nine hundred fifty dollars; gasoline was twenty-three cents per gallon; bread, eighteen cents a loaf, and a first-class postage stamp was three cents. The average yearly income was $4,137. Our home was modest, but our income level was well above most people.

Tougher times, however, were just around the corner. At Charlotte Textile Engravers I didn't report directly to Mr. Scala. My immediate superior was an older fellow, maybe thirty-five or forty. I was still in my mid-twenties, a mere kid to him. The relationship between us did not always go well. His attitude was a case of the resentment I spoke of earlier. I got the impression he resented the special relationship I enjoyed with Mr. Scala, the owner of the company, and he thought this Harper kid was just going to keep moving up until one day he would be reporting to Ronnie Harper. No one ever said that, but I sensed it.

My immediate boss liked to find ways to remind me he was my superior. At one point Katherine and I planned a vacation to Miami to visit with Katherine's brother George. My boss, who worked in Charlotte, told me, "You can't go on vacation because you are too busy down there in Greenville." That actually wasn't true; he just wanted to be ugly. When the date for our vacation came around, we went ahead and took off for Miami.

While we were in Florida, my boss telephoned and said it was important for me to get to Atlanta right away because a customer had a problem that needed to be dealt with immediately. I shut down our vacation and Katherine and I drove to Atlanta. When we arrived there, the customer expressed some surprise that I would cut our vacation short for him. "You could have stayed a few extra days. We have a problem here, but it is not earth shattering," were his words. This customer was someone I considered a friend; we knew his family. He couldn't understand why I had been told to curtail my vacation.

After dealing with him, we continued on back to Greenville, only to find other plots had been launched against me. My supervisor had sent his assistant to fill in as manager of the Greenville plant while I was on vacation and had instructed him to make notes of everything he found wrong at the facility. He came up with a pile of little complaints. To Mr. Scala, in Charlotte, I may have been the kid on a pedestal, but at that point he was shown a virtual black book on me.

Mr. Scala then got involved and visited me at the Greenville plant and started asking questions about the operation. By then, in my mind, some of the shine had been rubbed off my mentor's character. I'd begun to question his intentions at times. And it really hurt my feelings when I discovered what had been going on in my absence. I had been putting in so many hours, trying to do my best, and I was fed up and burned out. I just said to heck with it. I do not need this. I am burned out. I am just leaving. Everything happened almost overnight. I decided I didn't need that job anymore. Thinking I could make the same kind of money somewhere else, I resigned. Mr. Scala later called Katherine and asked her to beg me to stay. I didn't. I thought I knew better.

My quitting turned out to be a big blunder. We really suffered financially as a result. Here I was, the sole breadwinner for a family of seven, and I did not have a job. For me, the whole episode was one of those crucial turning points in life, a building block in strengthening me, my wife, and our marriage. Those kinds of ordeals do build character. They are not always welcome, but they do build character.

Looking back now, forty-some years later, I still feel a tremendous debt of gratitude to Al Scala despite the way the job ended for me there in Greenville. He had his failings. Ten or twelve years later, his marriage broke up. I had always thought Al and Rae Scala had the perfect marriage. Here was a young couple who started this business and worked hard at it. She did not work in the business but was very supportive of him and his long hours and used to travel with him. To me, they were just a beautiful couple. They divorced around 1972. Mr. Scala called me one day and he said, "Ronnie, I guess you have heard Rae and I are separated." That was probably the only personal thing the guy had ever said to me, and I said, "I didn't know." He said, "She just got tired of my long hours." Well, I learned later it wasn't long hours; it was another woman, another woman, and another woman.

Still, he remained a formative influence in shaping the rest of my life. He had the ability to get the most out of an employee; but with me, I think, there was something special. He saw my potential and knew how to cultivate it. I rose in that organization faster than anyone else ever had. He was a fatherly figure who I was always a bit intimidated by, to the point where I would never ask any in-depth questions that were not job related. We didn't have personal conversations. He asked me at one point to call him "Al," and I had a difficult time making the transition. To me, he was always "Mr. Scala."

I liked his positive attitude. He'd hear about things going wrong, but it wouldn't take the smile off his face. He just was always ready to go. He was very successful and eventually had a facility in Mexico and one in Canada. Those dealings intrigued me and stayed with me, even if he did run into problems with his business partner in Mexico. He died a few years ago at age eighty, I believe. To me he remains someone who saw something in me I had not seen.

After I resigned from my position with Charlotte Textile Engravers, we stayed in Greenville for awhile. The following months were the first time in our marriage when we really ran into financial difficulties. We had the Oldsmobile station wagon, which was paid for and we were able to refinance it. We also had bought a small organ, and when we couldn't make the monthly payments, we asked if we could somehow stretch out the payments. The people were nice enough to let us return it. When I was making ten thousand dollars a year, we often had problems paying all the bills, but we always somehow managed. It was a big awakening for me to suddenly be without a good income.

The first job I came up with was selling World Book Encyclopedias door-to-door. I sold them for about three months. The experience was a real education for me. Selling door to door was a miserable life, even with a fine product like the World Book Encyclopedia. The way I remember my manager encouraging me to sell a set of encyclopedias was to knock on a door, and when people responded, not to tell them I was selling encyclopedias. I would ask, instead, if they had any children and if they wanted to be sure their children had the same opportunity to enhance their education that the kids down the street and the youngsters on the next block were getting. Of course the answer would be yes, and I was supposed to get my foot in the door before having told them what I was selling.

Once in the door, my job was to tell them that for only ten cents a day their child could have a complete set of World Book Encyclopedias. I didn't tell the customers what the total cost would be or that, with interest, they would be paying for those encyclopedias for the rest of their lives and still never pay off the costs of the whole set. I had a real problem with such tactics. Yes, it was a fine product, and if children actually read them they could learn a lot. But this sales tactic seemed unethical to me. I was very uncomfortable with it.

I did make some sales, nonetheless, but after a month I had to go to my boss and tell him, "I'm going to have to look for another job because I am not making enough money here." He said, "Well, Ron, don't worry. The money is going to come flooding in. It just takes time. How much do you need?" I said, "About two hundred fifty dollars." "No problem." He whipped his checkbook out and wrote me a loan for two hundred fifty dollars. The following month the same thing happened. Three months into my new job, I owed him seven hundred fifty dollars.

At the same time, I was being given awards and prizes—ribbons, plaques—for making sales, and tons of praise. My boss kept telling me I had lots of potential. But the job wasn't putting food on the table. I couldn't see the light at the end of the tunnel. I kept thinking to myself, "My God, here I owe this man seven hundred fifty dollars. If I stick around selling encyclopedias another month, my debt can only go up."

Like I said, selling door to door was a real learning experience for me. Ever since then the loss of a job scares me to death. And I don't just mean the prospect of my losing my job. I learned what it is like to be in the shoes of someone with a family to feed and not having a job, or having a job that pays far too little to make ends meet. As a result, I have never taken any delight in having to fire someone and I've always tried to avoid having to lay off workers.

I finally had to go to my boss and tell him I was going to have to look for another job because I just was not making enough money. Someone had told me about an opportunity to sell insurance, and I jumped at the chance. My old boss at World Book hounded me in the months following for repayment of the seven hundred fifty dollars I had borrowed, with threatening letters from his attorney. Eventually, I did repay it all, with money that was much needed to pay the rent and put food on the table.

The time I spent selling insurance did not work out much better for me. I went into the insurance business feeling like it was something I wanted to do. I enjoyed the training and the professional nature of the business. Three months into it, I realized I was about to run out of friends to talk with about buying insurance and knew selling policies would be an uphill battle from there. Then, I got a call from John Ladley, owner of Consolidated Engravers in Charlotte. After leaving Charlotte Textile Engravers, I had submitted my resume to my former competitors and was pleasantly surprised when he called. The opportunity was too good to turn down; I could go back to doing what I knew I was good at.

For the first few months at Consolidated Engravers, I stayed with Katherine's aunt, Edna Schneidt, and returned to my family in Greenville on the weekends. Later we were able to rent a place in Charlotte, an even smaller home than what we were accustomed to living in. We had five children and a sister-in-law, my brother Gary's first wife, Carol, living with us. Gary was in the Eighty-second Airborne, stationed in Fayetteville, North Carolina. About a year later, once our home in Greenville sold, and with the help of a GI loan, we were able to buy a twenty-two-hundred-square-foot house in Charlotte that was about twenty years old. The real estate guy wanted sixteen thousand five hundred dollars and said we needed to put seven hundred fifty dollars down. We didn't have that kind of money, but he told us to write the check and as soon as we got the GI loan he promised to tear the check up, which he did.

At Consolidated Engravers I started out as an assistant manager in their textile roll engraving department, an area I had nine years of experience in, with plenty of knowledge in the sales field as well. They started me out mostly supervising production work and doing some sales in North and South Carolina. Probably 80 percent of my job there was production/supervision, and the other 20 percent was sales.

On the production side, we would take in used copper printing cylinders and put them on machining lathes to clean off the used or damaged surfaces, then we would re-coat them for re-engraving. We also built new cylinders to meet requested specifications. I supervised fifteen to twenty workers.

When selling, I traveled North and South Carolina and visited the same customers, mostly fabric printers, I knew from my earlier job. Consolidated Engravers was a slightly larger company than Charlotte Textile Engravers, and a direct competitor. The company also produced anilox rolls for the flexographic printing market, a field I learned much more about later in my time with that company.

Mr. Ladley was a tall, good-looking man, about fifty years old when I first started working for him. He was an astute businessman and a commanding presence when he was in the room. He was a very different sort of person from Al Scala. You always knew where you stood with Mr. Ladley. He would almost never give you a compliment, but if he didn't like what you were doing, he would tell you. Unlike Mr. Scala, I don't think Mr. Ladley knew I was even married or had children—and he could have cared less. But there was no chance of his being superficial. For the most part, he stayed out of my business and let me do my job. I did not have a lot of contact with him. Though I respected him, he never was for me the kind of role model Mr. Scala was. If I had to work for one of the two of them now, I'd probably choose Mr. Ladley. At that early point in my life, however, even though I grew to question his motives, it was Mr. Scala who I admired and was most influenced by.

The plant housing Consolidated Engravers was a huge, old, former textile mill building on Twelfth Street, two blocks off Tryon Street. From the outside it looked like a castle, painted gray. It was a monstrous place. Early on, only about 25 percent of the building was used by Consolidated Engravers, but as the company grew, walls were torn out and floors were re-concreted.

In my early period overseeing production at Consolidated Engravers, I learned of another aptitude I had. Part of the operation, when I started working there, was on the second story of the old mill building. An elevator, only about two feet by two feet square, and probably six feet high, was used to move materials. We used to put copper cylinders in that elevator and run them up and down between the first and second floor. I sat at home a few evenings and drew up a sketch to move the whole operation downstairs, then did some measuring to confirm the equipment would all fit on the lower floor. I was a little apprehensive about presenting my plan to the boss, but I did. I had written it down and reduced it to sketches and so forth. He liked the idea. Within a two- to three-month period, the entire operation was moved downstairs as a result of my idea and plan.

I realized, following this experience, that there was a bit of hidden talent in me. I also realized if you present your plans and dreams to the right people and give them time to think about your notions, those dreams become part of them, and plans are more likely to be implemented. I was pleased, in that case, to see my scheme turned into a reality.

After a couple of years, the sales manager of the flexographic printing side of the company wanted me to join him in selling products. This was my first involvement with flexography and selling the anilox rolls used on flexographic printing presses. I quickly fell in love with flexography and my life took an exciting turn. My work become more interesting and I put behind me the financial distresses of a few years earlier.

The year was 1964. Lyndon Johnson was president. John F. Kennedy had been assassinated the year before. A new home cost about thirty thousand dollars. A new car could be purchased for twenty-three hundred dollars; milk was $1.05 a gallon; gasoline, twenty-five cents a gallon; bread, twenty-one cents a loaf, and a first-class postage stamp had reached a new high of five cents! The average yearly income was $5,807. Mine was nearly double that and I was having a great time earning it.

Since my life from this point forward became increasingly focused on working in the field of flexography, it might be helpful for me to briefly explain what flexographic printing is and how it differs from other forms of printing. I forget sometimes that most people are not yet familiar with this form of printing, even though it is increasingly widespread. Flexographic printing is a variation on letterpress printing, the earliest form of printing on presses. In both, the image to be printed is a negative raised relief (mirror image) and the process can be thought of as a rotary ink stamp. Whereas letterpresses in the early days generally used metal image plates mounted on a cylinder and the thick ink used was applied with a rubber roller, flexography uses flexible rubber or, in more recent times, photopolymer plates on the image cylinder and the high viscosity, fast drying inks are applied to the printing plate with an "anilox roll."

Anilox rolls, which became my specialty, are rollers with

a microscopic, dimpled surface (knurled into the cylinder when I first started) that picks up the ink. On some presses the anilox roll actually turns in a tray of ink. The excess ink is then scraped off with a "doctor blade," which acts like a razor or a squeegee, leaving only the ink that is in the dimpled cells of the anilox roll. When the anilox roll turns against the flexible, image-bearing plate cylinder, a "kiss impression" occurs, transferring the ink to the raised parts of the image plate, before it is finally transferred to the material being printed, known as the "substrate" in the industry. If the printing is being done in color, often six, or even up to ten image cylinders are synchronized to deliver the different colors to the exact position needed.

This printing process differs from gravure and offset printing, the two other competing printing processes. In gravure, a negative of the image to be printed is engraved onto a metal cylinder such that the image is composed of tiny dimple cells and the non-image areas of the cylinder remain smooth. The cylinder turns in a tray of ink and then a doctor blade removes the excess ink, leaving only the ink in the tiny dimple depressions. Next, the cylinder presses against the substrate, leaving a positive print.

Offset printing, also known as lithography, is a bit more complex. Thick ink is massaged through a series of rubber rollers to achieve the desired thin film of ink, which then is rolled against a positive-image plate cylinder. Plates in offset printing are chemically treated such that the ink adheres to the engraved image on the plate and is repelled by the non-image areas. The ink is then "offset" onto another rubber "blanket cylinder," which in turn presses the image onto the paper or other substrate.

For many years flexography was the least popular of these forms of printing. It started back in the 1920s and up into the 1950s was known as aniline printing, because the inks used

1998 Ron and Katherine Harper

2002 Disney Cruise: *"Five children, thirteen grandchildren, two sons-in-law, and two daughters-in-law, plus Kat and I. A proud moment for us."*

Front row, l. to r.: Tony Ehrenberg, Natalie Harper, Lydia Kluttz, Christina Harper, Nathan Harper, Erica Kluttz, Londyn Ehrenberg, Dylan Ehrenberg. Back row: Hal Kluttz, Margie Kluttz, Lee Kluttz, Art Ehrenberg, Georgia Ehrenberg, Ron Harper, Katherine Harper, Lynn Harper, Danny Harper, Benjamin Harper, Isabela Harper, John Harper, Christopher Harper, Jim Harper, Jason Harper. (Inserted: Baby Raphael Harper, who was not born at the time. Born in May 2003.)

The United States Capitol, James H. Cromartie, artist
1986 First major painting of the U.S. Capitol, commissioned by Ron & Katherine Harper,
currently on display at Harper Corporation of America, Charlotte, N.C.

L. to R.: Grandson, Jason Harper; Ron and Katherine Harper; Senator Terry and Margaret Rose Sanford; Grandson Lee Klutz

"Kat and I spent many happy times with Senator and Mrs. Sanford in Washington D.C."

With appreciation for your friendship
and with best wishes always — to
Ron and Katherine Harper ~ Terry Sanford
U.S.S.

were made from aniline dyes, derived from indigo. These inks were smelly and noxious to work with and eventually were determined to be unhealthy, which, for awhile, gave this type of printing a bad reputation. A switch was made to solvent-based inks and, later, water-based inks. In 1957, the name was changed to flexography by the newly founded Flexographic Technical Association. The new name, derived from the use of flexible image plates, was an attempt to put the past behind. The name of the ink "pad" rollers known as anilox rolls retains the association with aniline.

When I moved into sales for the flexographic anilox department at Consolidated, my field of operation grew from the Carolinas to the whole United States. I traveled about every other week and found the air travel to be enjoyable. It was an exciting time for me. One week I'd go to Los Angeles. Next, I would visit Dallas, then other key areas of the country. Most of these places I had never been to before. I used to bring home pages of the newspapers from the different cities I visited. I really, really loved what I was doing, and absolutely fell in love with flexography, the process and the people.

I was primarily selling anilox rolls to package and label printers, the people who print labels on Carnation milk cans, Campbell's soup cans, and so forth. I sold to companies known as converters, that is, people who convert plastic or paper into a label and wrapper by printing it and shaping it. Corrugated box makers are converters, for example, printing on paper that gets converted into boxes. When you walk into a supermarket, about 70 percent of the labels and packaging you see was printed flexographically. Flexography is popular in this market because it is less expensive and faster process than other forms of printing.

We had a quality product, but it required someone to be in the field working with customers on their specifications, making sure they ordered the right specification for their kind of printing. I'd follow up after a week of traveling by making sure our production personnel were processing the orders correctly. I did a tremendous amount of follow-up work, making phone calls, checking on customers' jobs, planning the next week's travel.

I learned when I started working in the flexographic printing market that I was dealing with managers who spent more time studying their process and jobs. To me they seemed to be more educated about what they were doing and, therefore, more pleasant to work with. I liked that part and would try to do my best to satisfy them.

Another lesson I learned was how important it is to keep one's boss informed of what one is doing and how the assigned tasks are going. I didn't do it by boasting, but would let him know on a weekly basis how my job was progressing by submitting a written report. In those days, most of these reports were handwritten. They were then typed and were four to five pages long. I'd give them to my direct superior. He may never have read them, but the reports were at least in the file. I had informed him about what was happening and had taken the time to document what I had been up to. If he took a few minutes to scan a report, he could see we were making progress, and then ultimately the sales and revenues in the division would tell him whether I was doing a good or poor job. We did not have fifteen salesmen, so the bulk of the results were something I should have gotten credit or blame for, whichever the case may have been.

Things went well for me at Consolidated Engravers for nearly ten years before I was abruptly terminated. How it came about still baffles me. Before I started selling the anilox rolls, the sales manager of the flexographic department, a nephew of Mr. Ladley, was the only salesperson in that department. When I joined him, he started relaxing his work habits. He would show up at nine in the morning and take off at two in the afternoon to get his suit fitted and that sort of thing. I picked up the slack and did a good job, keeping track of my sales figures. Confident of my good performance, I came to him and asked if I could get a small raise. I was making twelve thousand dollars a year and my family was enjoying a good standard of living. But I was also working hard and thought I deserved a raise. He said he would speak with his direct superior about it.

I flew out to St. Louis for a week and was in touch with my sales boss by telephone on Wednesday. He asked, "Ron, when are you coming home?" I said, "Friday afternoon; I should be in before too late." He asked if I could come home a day early and I said, "Yeah, I guess so." So I did.

Having asked for a raise, I thought, "If they are pulling me off the road a day early, it must be pretty important. Maybe I am going to get a promotion." Well, shockingly, I got fired. The explanation at the time was, "Ron, we just cannot afford two salespeople. We are really sorry, but we are going to have to let you go." They offered me a job in Nigeria, where they had some little program going on, but I had no interest at all. Anyway, they turned me loose.

Once I recovered from my shock, I went over to Charlotte Textile Engravers to have a talk with my old boss and mentor, Al Scala. I wasn't looking for a job with him because I had already been offered a position with a company in Louisville, Kentucky. I wanted his advice and needed his encouragement. He tried to dissuade me from moving to Louisville, saying, "Ronnie, before you make your decision, I want to talk to you, because we are going to get into anilox roll engraving, we are going to get into flexography, and I am personally going to spend time getting it going."

He talked me into going to work for him again, but he did not get into flexography, which is what I really wanted to continue doing. For eighteen months I worked for him and he made no move to open up a flexographic department. That was a rare period in which I hated going to work every day. It was just bad. I kept dreaming of something better.

My life took another turn when I got a call from the general manager of the company that had fired me, Consolidated Engravers. He said, "Ron, your former supervisor has gone now and has taken a position in New England, and we need a replacement for him. Do you have any idea who would be interested?" I said I would. It was obvious to me they wanted me back. So I was fired as a sales representative, and hired as a sales manager. That development made the firing a year-and-a-half earlier a little easier to take.

I was back at the job I had enjoyed doing, traveling the country selling anilox rolls to converters. By then I was approaching forty and had plenty of experience behind me. In addition, I had developed confidence in myself and my ability to market a product. Other ideas were slowly beginning to percolate in my mind.

I was thinking about some sort of ownership of a company. I spoke with Mr. Ladley about maybe buying some stocks in Consolidated Engravers so I could have more of a vested interest and be able to share in the success of the company. About two months later, he got back to me. He said he had a block of stock that had opened up and he would be willing to sell it to me at a cost of "only" fifty thousand dollars. He may have been sincere, but I was insulted. I was only making about thirteen thousand dollars a year and supporting a family. I had expected some kind of workable plan; there was no way I could have come up with fifty grand. So my dreams of company ownership began drifting in other directions. Plus, more had been going on in my life besides work and some of my involvements had started to give me new and bigger ambitions.

During this period of my life, I did, for a brief time, become interested in spiritual matters. Ten years after Katherine and I were married, I joined the Catholic Church. This was when our children were attending the Catholic school. I got into the habit on my way home from work of stopping at the church, St. Patrick Cathedral, three or four times a week. I would just drop by and sit in a pew and meditate for a moment. Those moments, for me, were accompanied by a wonderful feeling.

Later, I went on a weekend retreat sponsored by the Church that sort of turned me off. I reverted to my more practical outlook, believing God helps those who help themselves. I believe there is a God; I do not question that at all. Nonetheless, I have never sat around and waited for God to do something for me and I do not recall ever praying for God to do me a favor. My interest beyond that waned and I haven't been inside a Catholic Church during the last fifteen years unless it was to attend a wedding or funeral.

Katherine is extremely spiritual. She reads extensively and most of what she reads has a spiritual theme to it. She can sit and talk about God, Christ, angels, and so forth for hours. Our outlooks have always been different. She was sure from the beginning our marriage was made in heaven. I thought it had to do more with our being willing to make a commitment to each other. When we unexpectedly received, just before the birth of our first baby, three hundred dollars from the U.S. Marine Corps for my "overseas" duty, Katherine was convinced it was divine intervention. I was as surprised as she was when the check arrived, but I viewed it as money I had earned and deserved.

For both of us our relationship to the Catholic Church has changed over the years. After six children, five of which survived, we decided to use birth control, something the church still disapproves of, though many Catholics have done as we have. Both of us were bothered by the way the church acted inconsistently at times. Katherine's brother George had a failed wartime marriage in the 1940s that had lasted about a year. He was very close to the church yet had to wait thirty years to get an annulment. He never did remarry. We'd pick up the newspaper and read about some celebrity getting an annulment from the church after just a year or two. Those kinds of grievances added up. We did insist our children go to Mass every Sunday up until they were sixteen years old. Then we let them make their own decision about spiritual matters. We are not anti-Catholic; we are just not practicing Catholics. Nonetheless, our involvement with the church and, particularly, the Catholic school in town, did give us new ideas that eventually led to us launching our own company.

When our children were attending the O'Donahue Catholic school, we got involved in a way that awakened our imaginations to new possibilities not just for the school but for our own future in business. Katherine was the president of the Home School Association, the Catholic school's version of the PTA. While serving in that capacity, she noticed the books in the school library were almost all out of date. History books were thirty years old. This was the late 1960s and the history books on China still had Chiang Kai-shek as the premier, which hadn't been true since the mid-1940s. Katherine decided to raise money to buy new books for the library.

We came up with the idea of sponsoring a dinner dance, charging about five or six dollars for a steak dinner and having a twenty-one piece band provide dance music. We had flyers printed up to get the word out, made phone calls, and talked enthusiastically about the upcoming event to everyone we met. We informed people about the need to get updated books for the children at the school and told them how they could help by participating. The first dinner dance had a cowboy theme. We called it the "Brush Poppers Ball." We told guests to don their cowboy attire and come prepared for a good time. The event was a tremendous success. Probably half of the four hundred people who came were Catholics and the other half were Protestants. Our guests had a good time, as did Katherine and I.

Over the next few years, we sponsored three more similar events. Ty Boyd, a local radio celebrity at the time, agreed to be master of ceremonies for one of these Brush Poppers Balls and we were able to get the Loonis McGlohon band to entertain and provide dance music. The Holiday Inn Central Charlotte was the only hotel in the late 1960s that could accommodate the group we attracted. Half the price of admission went to pay for the food, drinks, and entertainment, plus the use of the hotel ballroom. The other half was designated for the purchase of new books for the school library.

The money was turned over to the priest, and we later learned some of it was used to pave an expanded parking lot so the church could have more spaces for bingo. Using the money for something other than what it was raised for didn't go over well with us and was another one of those grievances that drove a wedge between us and the church. Still, we look back on the whole experience of having sponsored those fundraisers as a significant eye-opener for us.

What fund-raising made us realize was how effective we could be putting a project together, marketing an idea, organizing an event, and enjoying watching it all come to pass. At that point the idea of starting our own company was born. Little did we know what that would eventually lead to.

Our third home

"Our dream began in a back room on August 2, 1971, and took off. I was thirty-eight-and-a-half years old (almost 'over the hill'). We started as Ron Harper Associates, Ltd. and, in 1975, changed the name to Harper Corporation of America."

CHAPTER THREE

Harper Corporation of America

In 1971, I was working for Consolidated Engravers and learning thirteen thousand dollars. Katherine was bringing in a second paycheck, working at Wachovia Bank. We were buying our home and had five children, plus Katherine's mother and my nephew Steve (who my parents adopted after I had grown up) living with us. We have an enlarged photo of the home we were living in at that time (a gift from a friend, Charlie Lockhart) in the front lobby of our business headquarters in Charlotte, not to show our humble beginnings in contrast to where we are now, but to remind ourselves we were content back then. We were doing okay.

Some people go into business because they want to make tons of money. They have heard you can't make real money working for someone else. Others start their own business because they want to control their work schedule. Neither of these reasons motivated us. Our motivation was that we felt we had the ability to market a product and satisfy customers, and we wanted to prove to ourselves we could.

We like to remind ourselves we did not start a business because we wanted to increase our income. Money really was a secondary concern. We went into business because we had a burning desire to try something on our own. Based on the confidence we had developed during the marketing we had done for the Catholic school, we felt sure we could succeed on our own and we were eager to try.

Money, we figured, would come from the effort. But, honestly, when we first went into business, one of my concerns was we might get rich someday. As a young man, I had always thought a person had to be a little devious to be successful in business. I didn't want to be that way and I feared what success might do to me.

The ideas for the new business evolved slowly. At one point we looked at a picture-framing business and traveled to Raleigh and Atlanta checking out franchise possibilities. Then a friend of ours said, "If you are going into business, you really need to go into a business you understand and know something about; getting into something new and different is dangerous." We were terribly naive at that time, but that statement was pretty important to us. We started considering where our expertise lay and what the possibilities might be in those fields. For me, my expertise lay in manufacturing and marketing cylinders for printing presses.

Katherine and I discussed our options over a period of time before making a decision. I always worked long hours, and often on a Sunday afternoon, I would be doing work on our dining room table, following up on the past week or planning the next week. I began to feel guilty if I was working for my employer on Sunday afternoon and not our new business idea. If I worked on the new business, I felt guilty because I knew people were paying me to do a job and I was not attending to their business. Nonetheless, preparations took time. Finally, I realized if we were going to be serious about starting our own venture, I had to leave my job and devote myself full time to the new business.

One of the first things we did was to buy a new 1971

Impala Chevrolet because we felt there had to be an appearance of success in our new business venture. In addition, we had saved up about one thousand dollars, and we had a Master Charge credit card to get started with. There was a small room in the back of our home, in which we installed a separate telephone line for the business. The twenty-nine dollar

1969 Kat and Ron at the American Hotel in New York
City, attending an FFTA Annual Conference
"A happy time in the city."

deposit for the second phone was part of our initial outlay of cash. We also bought a little, wooden, used desk to place the phone on and we were in business, though we weren't altogether sure what direction we were going with the business.

In August of 1971, on a Monday, we opened. To let our friends in the industry know I was in business, we chose the name Ron Harper Associates Ltd., for the new company. The Associates part indicated it was more than just me, as Katherine would be working part time, and I thought the Ltd. part would give the business an international flair.

Soon after launching, we opened up the American Metal

Service Division, and the American Maintenance Service Division—all located in that one little room and run from our little school desk. I knew there was a demand for basic, non-engraved metal cylinders that Consolidated Engravers and textile plants purchased and engraved for use on printing presses. In the past I had been involved in subcontracting the production of such cylinders to local machine shops. I figured I could become an independent contractor for these cylinders, working with the same machine shops I'd worked with in the past, then sell the cylinders to textile plants and to my old employer, Consolidated Engravers. I already had the contacts and network for selling the end product and immediately got off to a good start in the metal service division. We didn't manufacture anything ourselves. Everything we sold, we subcontracted. But what we did sell, we sold under our name.

The American Maintenance Service division was really a fancy name for what never got beyond a simple house-painting business. We invested in a truck and put to work a friend of ours who lived two doors up the street. This fellow was kind of a handyman who knew how to paint and do minor repair work and home additions. He started out as a partner in that division. The only problem was he had a hard time estimating how much paint would be required to paint a house and what the costs would be. After he painted just a couple of houses, we were already losing serious money. The house owners would insist on a second coat and he had only estimated the cost of one coat. It seemed prudent for us to get out of that line of work and we told our friend he could borrow the truck and try to make it on his own. He only lasted a few more weeks. We closed the division.

The demise of that division was matched with the beginning of a new division shortly thereafter, a more profitable one and a source of steady income for us. Most of the credit has to go to Katherine. She was working as a bank teller and had a customer from a chemical company who came in weekly to make a deposit. The two of them would chat about his business. One day she talked to him about the need in the printing industry for a cleaner that could remove dried ink from printing rollers and other machine parts. Anilox rolls, in particular, with the little ink cells on the surface, pose a difficult problem when it comes to cleaning them. If ink dries in the bottom of the cells, the efficiency of the inking process can be severely affected. The products available at that time did not do an adequate job. He expressed an interest, and I took him some metal parts that had ink hardened on them. Within a few weeks, after experimenting and testing different solutions, he came up with a product that worked wonderfully.

The chemical company began producing the anilox roll cleaner for us in powder and liquid forms. The company put the cleaner in drums, put our label on the drums, and stored it for us. In the early days, we sold the cleaner over the phone primarily to flexographic printing companies, mostly people I knew, and we saw quick acceptance of our product. We only had to market the cleaner, and when we made a sale we would simply pick up the phone and call the chemical company and say, "Ship a load to this company at this address."

During the early years of our company, the steady income this cleaning solution brought in helped tremendously. We were paying twenty-eight dollars a drum for it, ready to ship, and we were selling it for about $133, a very competitive price at the time. We were making good money, with a high profit margin. Before long, selling that product was bringing in fifteen thousand dollars a month and it continued to sell around that level for over twenty-five years.

The Metal Service Division of our company also became successful, but progress was not as smooth and easy. When I worked for Consolidated Engravers, part of my job was to put together the required specifications and order from local machine shops the rollers and other elements that were needed in the production process. We would then do the engraving on the rollers and send them on to our customers. I just took that knowledge and networking and proved to the people at Consolidated early on that I could supply them with the same quality, non-engraved cylinders for the same or less than they had been purchasing cylinders in the past. The big advantage for Consolidated Engravers was I would save them the trouble of having to negotiate with the various machine shops.

The people at Consolidated, my main customer, welcomed my service for about four months before they sensed I could turn into a competitor and they cut me off, hoping to put me out of business. This move might have been disastrous for our new venture had it not been for an unforeseen development. Already, by early December, we had hired a salesperson to help expand our market. We sent this fellow to a convention in Minneapolis, and he came back to tell us about someone in Portland, Oregon who had come up with an innovation in the manufacturing of anilox rolls. Rather than using the standard chrome plating on the rolls, there had been some demonstrated success in using a ceramic coating.

That development got me thinking. I had a non-compete agreement with Consolidated for one year after leaving, specifying I could not coat or engrave chrome cylinders. If ceramic was substituted for the chrome coating, I would not be violating that agreement, as I would be offering a qualitatively different product, though one that served the same purpose.

The next step was to find someone who could provide the kind of ceramic coating required. We needed to be able to apply a ceramic coating in a way that was much more complex than merely painting on a coat of liquid ceramic and then baking it in a kiln. We were looking for what is known as plasma flame spray technology. A very fine ceramic powder is blown at high pressure through a thermal flame spray gun that basically encircles the sprayed powder with an intense, twelve thousand-degree-Fahrenheit flame, melting the powdered ceramic, which then gets blasted onto the cylinder. To get an even application, the cylinder needs to be revolving as the spray gun traverses down the length of it. The high-pressure application increases the density and hardness of the ceramic coat. The result is a coating that is much more durable than chrome, thus capable of withstanding longer wear, and also capable of being engraved more precisely.

We looked around Charlotte and Atlanta for a place with this kind of plasma flame spray technology, without success. About a month later, I found a company, almost by accident, right here in Charlotte. Ceramco was an industrial ceramic company specializing in applying ceramic to water pumps, cylindrical parts, or any metal item needing protection from abuse, corrosion, or impact damage. Doing a friend a favor one day, my son Jimmy and I dropped off a measuring device there and found three guys in the front office playing cards. These three were the owners, who had just opened for business the month before.

The three men were willing to work with us to develop and produce the kind of product we wanted to be able to sell. I knew if I could offer a superior anilox roll, I could use my extensive experience in selling rolls to companies across America to quickly expand our new company. Together with the people at Ceramco, we did a lot of development work, doing research on a small, but intense, scale. Precision in the application was needed to get uniform coatings with specific depths. Our efforts paid off and we signed a three-year contract with Ceramco and began production. We were the second in the world to coat ceramics on cylinders for the purpose of engraving them for use in flexographic printing. And, while we were the second to get into this technology, we were the first to have any real success in selling these new products.

Our success did not just happen overnight or come without a lot of hard work. At the beginning, I really was not interested in getting into manufacturing. I knew my strengths were in sales. If I could subcontract the production and then sell the product, I hoped I could stay clear of the hassles that come with operating and maintaining equipment in a production environment. I still had to negotiate with the machine shops making the cylinders that were to be coated with ceramic, then arrange for the cylinders to be transported from one locale to the other. Ceramco, meanwhile, though it had the plasma flame spray equipment, did not have the kind of lathe-like turning equipment that was needed to apply the ceramic to larger cylinders and then to polish the finished products to the precise specifications required before engraving them.

In trying to overcome the difficulties involved, I was drawn more and more into manufacturing. First, we needed a larger facility in which to do the ceramic coating on large rolls. Ceramco did not have room at its plant. We leased a five-thousand-square-foot space in a large building on Crompton Street, just off Westinghouse Boulevard, in Charlotte, and purchased a large lathe needed for turning the cylinders. Later we ended up buying our own truck to get past the difficulties we were experiencing in transporting cylinders, where we had been having to bear the costs of all too frequently damaged cylinders.

Despite the difficulties, we did get started, turning out our new product. The competition berated this new product, being unaware of the advantages a ceramic coating offered and underestimating my determination. In selling the new rollers, I would remind customers of how easy it is to damage a chrome cylinder. "A baby with a teaspoon," I'd say, "could damage the surface of a chrome roll, but not a ceramic roll." Ceramic can be damaged, but it is much more forgiving of abuse. And it lasts longer.

We were successful because I was familiar with the anilox roll market and flexography in general. I had sold to most of these same people in the past and could now offer them a superior product. The company in Oregon that first developed ceramic-coated anilox rolls did not have these advantages and did not fully understand marketing. Some people think if you turn out a good product, word of mouth will spread and the world will come knocking at your door. Marketing doesn't work this way. Our product was superior, but even then, we only had an edge over competitors because of our marketing expertise. I have always said you can build a better mousetrap, but unless you have the willingness and ability to tell the world about it, nobody is going to beat a path to your door. We had the know-how to do the marketing, and the desire, and we got off to a good start.

By then we had also opened up another division in the company, in part because my brother Dick had joined us. Dick had been working for Celanese Corporation in Cumberland, Maryland, where our dad used to work. At one point he was given the assignment of coming down to inspect the Celanese operation Rock Hill, South Carolina, and while carrying out the task he stayed in our home. We suggested he ought to join us and work with us. He agreed and returned to Cumberland to give notice that he was resigning from Celanese. Then he and his wife, Norma, moved to Charlotte. He had saved up eleven thousand dollars and was willing to invest his money in the company in exchange for a 5 percent share of the business. With Dick on board, and given his penchant for working with machines, we started refurbishing equipment of all kinds.

Dick's division was successful enough that we spun it off and incorporated it as a separate company, which we named

Harper Machinery Corporation. A little later, with Dick running the operation, it just seemed appropriate to make the division his company. He ended up buying our shares and has been in business now for over twenty-five years, and has done extremely well.

Meanwhile, when our three-year contract with Ceramco expired early in 1975, we decided to take charge of the manufacturing part of the business ourselves and, thereby, increase our control over the quality of the end product. I had hoped to avoid having to do so, but we ran into problems and taking over the manufacturing ourselves seemed, at the time, to be the best solution. As I have said, I never had an urge or burning desire to go into manufacturing. I have always been a salesman, a marketing person. I like the suit-and-tie part of the business. Taking over the manufacturing greatly increased my workload. I had to hire new people, buy new equipment, and oversee the operation, as well as continue to market the product nationally and, increasingly, internationally.

When we took over the manufacturing process, we assumed full control of the operation on Crompton Street and continued to expand. We had originally leased five thousand square feet in a twenty-eight-thousand-square-foot building. Every time a tenant moved out, we grabbed his space, so eventually we had the whole building. Even that, before long, proved to be inadequate for our growing needs. Not only were we engraving anilox rolls, we were by then offering refurbishing services as well.

It was at this point, in 1975, that we changed the name of the company to Harper Corporation of America, feeling the old name, Ron Harper Associates Ltd., projected too small an image. The progress we had made in manufacturing and marketing ceramic anilox rolls had opened up much greater opportunities for growth and market expansion.

114

This period was an exciting time for me. From my office I could see the loading docks. When one of the dock doors opened and I saw a tractor trailer bringing in a roll for reconditioning from a customer, I was the first one out of the office, the first one to the truck, because I was excited to see a customer had sent us another roll for repair. I had most of our customers in my head and I would want to know who had sent us business. Those were thrills for me.

In the early years of our business Katherine did the bookkeeping, while continuing to work part time as a teller at a bank. She took care of the bills and dealt with the financing. This arrangement worked well, because I had little in the way of financial experience and, of course, when people lack a financial background, they generally don't recognize their own weakness. I thought if something cost fifty cents and we sold it for a dollar, we made fifty cents. It took me a while to realize if something costs me fifty cents and I sell it for a dollar, I haven't made fifty cents until I get paid. I have to admit, I didn't really understand the notion of "receivables" until about ten years ago.

Katherine would fuss if we didn't have as much money in the bank as she felt we should, and she wouldn't say anything if we did. She wouldn't tell me because I would go spend the money. There was a case where I learned we had ten thousand dollars in the bank and I picked up the phone and bought a new piece of equipment, so there went the ten thousand dollars. I had much to learn. We had to pay salaries and wages long before we were getting paid back. I had to learn about cash flow. Then someone told me once that some really successful, fast-growing companies go bankrupt because they run out of cash. These companies are successful to the point where all their money is tied up in receivables, inventory, and so forth. Fortunately for me, I had Katherine. I could not have succeeded without her. She is the one who would arrange for short-term loans from different banks, made sure all the bills were paid, then as quickly as possible got the loans paid off.

The manufacturing of ceramic-coated anilox rolls became our hallmark, but we also continued to produce chrome rolls to meet a persisting demand. Chrome rolls were less expensive and one will always find customers looking for the cheapest deal. The chrome rolls remained popular for use in printing some finished products, particularly among manufacturers of corrugated boxes. In addition, we produced and sold glue applicator rolls used in the production of corrugated boxes. Business was going well for us in the manufacturing department, plus, by then, we had launched another company that was bringing in handsome profits.

As was evident to us in the success we had marketing cleaning solutions, some of the best business is to be found in the manufacturing and selling of mundane products that are essential. When I was a young man, probably in my mid- to late twenties, a fellow down the street owned a fancy new Cadillac. Curious as to how he made his money, I asked someone what he did for a living. I was told he was a button salesman, marketing to department stores and fabric shops. I was absolutely astounded at how much money a person can make in certain niches. He became an inspiration to me: Someone can make a good living selling buttons. I just thought, if he can do it, so can I, if I can just find the right niche.

The cleaning solution turned out to be one of those niches that worked out well for us and we were on the lookout for other opportunities. Another came along in 1978. By then Harper Corporation of America had a well-established reputation internationally. We were the company that first successfully marketed ceramic-coated anilox rolls and our cleaning solutions were widely used. We had recently opened up a textile chemical department, hoping to develop some profitable new dye formulas, but were not having much success. Then, one of our salesmen,

Bob Elfner, while traveling in Australia and New Zealand, giving educational seminars, came across something he thought we might want to investigate.

An Australian company had developed an adhesive additive that it claimed was superior to anything else on the market. Basically, this was an additive for the glue that gets used to bind the little flutes in the production of corrugated cardboard. The glue with the additive developed by this company and being marketed around Australia was waterproof and faster drying than competing glues.

Bob called me from the airport in Sydney, asking if we would have an interest in producing and marketing corrugated adhesive additives in the United States. He was excited enough about the product that I agreed to meet with representatives from the company. Our reputation for effective marketing must have impressed the company's management team, because within thirty days the team was in Charlotte with a draft of a contract in hand.

We revised the contract over a weekend, hammering out further details in the formation of a partnership to be called Harper-Love Adhesive Corporation. The Love part was for Nigel B. Love, owner of the Love Company based in Sidney. Each partner put up six thousand dollars to begin marketing the adhesive product in the United States and agreed to loan another twenty-two thousand dollars to the new corporation a few months later.

Our recently opened textile chemical department and much of the mixing/blending equipment that went with it was converted over for use in the production of the adhesive additive. Harper Corporation sold the equipment to Harper-Love Adhesives. The Australians helped us set up the manufacturing, and by the end of the first year we were already making a profit.

This venture, engaging in something outside of our sphere of expertise, has been an extremely successful part of our business. Our original investment of six thousand dollars brought in substantial profits over the next twenty-five years. There ended up being a lot of money to be made in a glue product that most people would never give any thought to, something less visible than buttons. But I don't think our partnership with Love Adhesives would ever have occurred had it not been for our solid reputation for having strong marketing capabilities, nor would success have come about had we not followed through and persuasively sold the product.

Lest people think we at Harper have the Midas touch, let me comment on a few ventures that ended up being expensive education for us. In 1977, we thought we were ready to expand our operations and opened a plant in Chicago, as a second center for manufacturing anilox rolls. We leased a small facility and brought in equipment with plans to do what we were doing in Charlotte, but on a smaller scale. Chicago was a good market, and the objective was to expand from that original plant as soon as the demand warranted it.

The expansion did not go as planned. Our son Jimmy was given the job of managing the operation. We struggled for three years to turn a profit in a high-cost, high-turnover labor market. When the landlord doubled the rent, it was the straw that broke the camel's back. We shut the plant down, backed up a couple of tractor-trailer trucks, loaded up the equipment and brought it down to Charlotte. It would be seventeen years before we were able to reestablish a presence in the Midwest. This closure was a setback for us, but not the only one.

About the same time, we also attempted to expand our anilox roll manufacturing into the Los Angeles area by forming a loose joint venture with a fellow we had met at a trade conference. He worked in the machine shop environment in L.A. and seemed to know how to get things done. We liked him and thought with his help we could get started out there. He was very interested, and in the months following he bought the needed equipment, and we helped him get set up and taught his people how to produce anilox rolls.

In keeping with my original intention when starting our company, we planned, at least in this new venture, to let someone else do the manufacturing while we did the marketing. The terms of our agreement were that we would do most of the selling and earn royalties on the sales of the anilox rolls manufactured in his plant.

One of our salesmen, Carl Wagner, worked out of his plant and before long reported that sales of anilox rolls were being made surreptitiously, depriving us of the royalties to which we were entitled. A dispute followed and we refused to compromise on the issue and pulled out of the joint venture, even though this move left us with a competitor out in L.A., one we had essentially created. But without our marketing, the L.A. anilox business never got far and we faced little real competition down the road. For us this venture ended up being a lesson about the need to do our homework and why not to get involved with the wrong people. Fortunately, since we had not invested in any equipment ourselves, the losses were not substantial.

There was one other early failure that resulted mostly from my eagerness to keep expanding in business. For many years I had a burning desire to grow for growth's sake. I was far less concerned about the bottom line. I wanted to grow, and I thought the profits would come.

Our efforts in Chicago and L.A. did not fare well and I thought the problem was in trying to manage a business at a distance. We could do better, I thought, if we diversified right here in Charlotte, getting into something else but doing so nearby, where we could keep close tabs on the operation. Given our marketing expertise, I figured we could succeed at just about anything that way.

The first promising opportunity was presented to us by our financial auditors, who were also auditing the books of

Metal Service Corporation, a heating-and-air conditioning business located on Clanton Road and South Boulevard. The owner of the business was dying of cancer and seeking someone to buy him out.

Not wanting to delay negotiations until the man's death was imminent and appear to be taking advantage of him in his last days, I kind of rushed the negotiations and, again, did not complete the homework. We bought the company, which had the franchise for selling Westinghouse heating and air conditioning units for residences. Westinghouse was a well-known brand and we felt good about that. The former owner died a few weeks after the sale was complete.

Three months later, York Air Conditioning Company bought the Westinghouse Air Conditioning Division and discontinued our product line. Now, here was our new company, without a major product line to market. We struggled for a while before linking up with the Coleman Company, the outfit that makes lanterns, camping equipment, stoves, tents, and such. It had a small division for residential heating and air conditioning units and we took it on. Coleman is a well-known company but not in the heating and air conditioning business. Coleman gave us a well-known name but not a well-known product.

Most of our sales were to small-time contractors who would install the equipment. They were a different sort of customer from what we were accustomed to dealing with. Our customers were repeatedly late with payments and would give us excuses like, "My customer has not paid me; how can you expect me to pay you?" That style was something we weren't used to. We have never said that to one of our suppliers.

At any rate, we lost money on the venture every year for eight years before we finally sold the company. Business showed no indication of turning around. More important, we never fell in love with the business. We never felt like insiders, like movers and shakers in that market. We were dealing in a different market segment and we learned not only to do more thorough research before buying but also that we were not good at marketing to every sector. We probably hung on as long as we did because I just didn't want to deal with the issue; I didn't like hearing about it—until we got a little pressure from our financial advisers. They told us, "Look, give it away, sell it, bankrupt it, do something, but get rid of it. It is not doing anything for you." In the end, we sold the business.

Failures have been an education for me. The advantage, I realized, in owning a company is no one can fire me for making mistakes. There is a positive side to this. I remember how I used to admire Al Scala and John Ladley for their creative abilities in making decisions. It was years later before I understood they could exercise their choices because, as long as they could financially survive their mistakes, they could afford to make them. Here I can make mistakes if we can survive financially, but if I reported to a board of directors, I most likely would have been fired a long time ago. Still, I understand without the freedom to make errors in judgment, one doesn't learn and one is unwilling to take the kind of risks that are sometimes required in order to succeed. I have learned a great deal from my mistakes.

Success in other areas kept us going well. We moved into our new six-thousand-square-foot home in the Quail Hollow area of Charlotte in 1981. A few years later, with space limitations continuing to be a problem at our production plant on Crompton Street, we began looking around for a good area to relocate our business.

Katherine took the initiative in finding an architect and, with his help, searching for an appropriate site on which to build a new corporate headquarters and manufacturing plant.

A ten-acre parcel on Steele Creek Road in southwest Char-lotte interested her most. A Japanese firm owned the prop-erty. Katherine offered them about three-quarters of their ask-ing price and her offer was accepted.

Following the purchase of the property, we all worked together, including company employees from all departments, in designing a new facility. We talked at length with the ar-chitect about work flow, and he helped us develop a plan that would best move the production process along in a fifty-thou-sand-square-foot layout. Construction got under way in 1984, and we moved the manufacturing equipment in and went into operation in February of 1985. Two months later we moved our office staff into the new eleven-thousand-square-foot building that is now the company headquarters. When we first occupied the facility, the office space seemed humongous, but over time we have had to be creative in redesigning space to accommodate our growing demands.

The production and refurbishing of anilox rolls contin-ued to be our main source of income in the late 1980s. The process was much the same as what we do today, though there have also been major innovations. The manufacturing of the steel rolls and the shafts that attach to the ends of them are subcontracted to local machine shops. When they arrive at our shop there remains considerable work to be done. A stain-less steel coating, for example, is often added. Putting a stain-less steel coating on is done in a mechanical welding process that basically welds a bead of steel onto the cylinder as the cylinder is revolving and the welding apparatus is traversing the length of the cylinder. When the process is completed, the cylinder has to be put in a lathe and trimmed and polished to an exact diameter.

Next, the roll is transferred to the thermal spray apparatus where, as I described before, a high-pressure spray of pow-dered ceramic goes through an intense flame which melts the

ISO Certification at Harper Corp. Charlotte, NC
"This gave us world-class status."

ceramic powder just before it goes onto the roll. The roll revolves as the thermal spray gun traverses the length of it, applying an even coat of ceramic to the surface of the roll. Following that, the roll has to, again, be put in a lathe and be polished to a precise diameter.

Up until 1989, we continued to mechanically engrave the rolls, using a round milling tool, much like a knurling device. The tool would press into the roll under tremendous pressure as the roll and the tool rotated against each other and the milling tool moved down the length of the roll. The little, hardened, diamond-shaped protrusions on the milling tool would leave indentations on the roll. The protrusions were precisely engineered to create diamond-shaped dimples that would hold a predetermined amount of ink. Precision in the timing was all important, so the milling tool perfectly matched with the circumference of the roll and traversed at a rate that left precisely spaced indentations without any overlap.

Chrome plated rolls, which we continued to produce up until 1990, were engraved in much the same manner. Rolls returned for refurbishing is a big part of our business, since it is cheaper to restore a used roll than to buy a new one, undergo the same process. Generally, a roll needing refurbishing is first put in a lathe and the old ceramic or chrome coating, together with some of the underlying metal, is removed.

Then, to restore the correct diameter to the roll, the welding process is applied to build it back up. More lathe work follows before the ceramic coating is applied.

A significant innovation occurred in the manufacturing process in 1989 with the introduction of laser engraving. Union Carbide, a European company to begin with, now known as Praxair, manufactures, among other things, anilox rolls. That company was the first to introduce the use of laser machines to engrave anilox rolls. The Union Carbide licensee in the United States, Pamarco, one of our biggest competitors at the time, brought the technology into this country but did not aggressively market it. The company boasted about its new technology but seemed content, for the most part, to stick with the mechanical engraving of chrome and ceramic rolls. It seemed to have no incentive to switch over as they were doing well with the status

1979 Katherine and Ron in Harper Corp's manufacturing
plant, watching an anilox roll turn in a lathe
*"This photo was taken for an article in the
old Charlotte News newspaper."*

quo. Union Carbide, a few years later, revoked Pamarco's license and began operations in the United States itself, promoting laser-engraved ceramic anilox rolls.

Before long I recognized the revolutionary implications of this new technology for our industry. I realized that to stay competitive we would have to embrace the new method, and the sooner we could do so the more Harper Corporation would get publicized as an innovative leader.

There were two companies building the kind of laser equipment we would need to engrave anilox rolls. One was named Basil, based in Germany, though that company later sold its laser division to a company in England. The second company was Zed, based in England. Union Carbide was getting lasers from Basil. We did our research and decided to do business with Zed because we thought its machines did a better job and it offered better service. Over the years, we have acquired nineteen of these machines, mostly from Zed, though we have four from the other companies. Different models handle different size anilox rolls and engrave at varying parameters. They cost over a half-million dollars each.

Our relatively new manufacturing facility, nicely laid out to maximize work-flow efficiency, was not big enough to accommodate the large new laser machines, some of which are twenty-five feet long and require ten to twelve feet of width. We added a large wing to our new plant. By December of 1989, we had laser equipment installed and we turned out our first ceramic-coated, laser-engraved roll.

The laser machines resemble, in some ways, large, modern-looking lathes. The ceramic coated rolls revolve in the machines. A laser beam apparatus directs a pulsating beam at a roll from several inches away. Pulsating at twelve thousand hits per second, the laser beam burns little dimples, called cells, one at a time in the ceramic coating by melting the ceramic material and pushing the molten material to the sides. As the roll revolves, the laser beam slowly traverses the length of it, taking up to twenty-four hours to complete the engraving process on a large, twenty-foot long roll.

When we first began using laser technology, six hundred cells per linear inch were considered fine screen-print quality. The early laser beams burned a diamond-shaped cell, laid out at a forty-five degree angle to the axis of the roll, much like the mechanical engraving-milling tool pressed into the ceramic. The biggest contribution Harper Corporation has made to the flexographic printing industry lies in the research we did into improving anilox cell structures and introducing a new engraving pattern, as well as increasing the number of cells per inch.

Our son Chris deserves much of the credit for coming up with this innovation. He was working for us at that point, directing research and development. Chris calculated that if the cells on an anilox roll were shaped like a hexagon rather than a diamond, 15 percent more cells could fit into a square inch. The hexagonal, honeycomb-like pattern is a more efficient use of space.

In looking at an anilox roll with the naked eye, one does not see the complex cell pattern but only a slightly rough surface, like a very fine grindstone. Anyone unaware of the engraving process would be surprised at the intricacy of the surface. The cells on an anilox roll are minute, requiring a microscope to inspect the quality of a cell's structure. A human hair is, on average, about seventy microns in diameter. There are 24,400 microns in an inch. The cell widths on an anilox roll can be designed to be less than twenty microns across when engraved with a laser beam. Yet, minute changes in the parameters of those tiny cells significantly affect the quality of printing in flexography.

The volume of ink a cell on an anilox roll can hold is critical to the printing process. Different materials being printed on require varying amounts of ink, depending on how much the material absorbs the ink. Anilox rolls are custom designed with different cell sizes and depths for different applications in the printing process. Each cell will deposit a little droplet of ink onto the image plate. The smaller the droplets, the quicker they will be absorbed into the substrate and dry, and the faster the printing presses can run.

Another critical factor is how efficiently the cells release the ink onto the flexible image plate. Chrome anilox rolls remained popular as long as they did partly because the chrome material was less porous than ceramic and the ink didn't cling to the chrome as much, thus producing a more efficient transfer of ink. Innovations in ceramic materials have changed the ink-transfer equation, and so have changes made in the design of the cells. Shallower cells release the ink better than deeper cells.

The implications of the introduction of the hexagonal pattern were significant. An anilox roll could carry more ink with the new pattern. Better yet, the cells can be shallower and still carry the same amount of ink and more of the ink will transfer. The result is a smoother lay down of ink, leading to better quality printing and less problems cleaning the ink out of the cells of a roll after a job is completed.

Research continued in this department. We also determined that arranging the pattern of the hexagonal cells at sixty degrees to the axis of the roll eliminated potential streaking. And we did numerous experiments to determine the optimum cell width to depth ratios.

Harper Corporation began using laser engraving technology in December of 1989. In mid-1990 we introduced the new cell pattern design, having fitted new laser beam emitters onto our laser engravers. Our attempts to patent these innovations failed, and before long others copied our success. The hexagonal cell pattern became the standard in the industry. Harper Corporation, however, received credit and considerable attention in all the publicity accompanying the change.

In addition to the new, innovative cell pattern, we began experimenting with increasing the number of cells per linear inch, aiming for even greater definition in flexographic print quality. From six hundred cells per inch, we almost immediately introduced eight hundred, then nine hundred, and then twelve hundred. We have turned out as many as two thousand cells per inch in a production roll, though most of what we do is somewhere between eight hundred and one thousand. The quality of flexographic printing has dramatically improved as a result. When printing on the same type of paper, flexographic printing, including six-color and ten-color presses, can now compete for quality with the best in offset printing.

The hexagonal cell configuration was a huge innovation and little has been done to modify the results of our research done in the early 1990s. But we did not stop searching for other ways to improve the product we manufacture. The next big innovation we came up with was the "platinum anilox roll," developed by our son-in-law, Art Ehrenberg, at our newly opened Green Bay, Wisconsin facility. Fortunately, the research on this product was completed in time for us to start producing and marketing the platinum roll in the year 2000, right when the economic downturn would have begun hurting our business. The superior quality of this product gave us an edge over the competition and total sales have grown 13 1/2 percent in the past year despite economic hard times.

Since we have had little success in the past in getting patents for our innovations, we have learned to depend more on trade secrets and confidentiality agreements to retain exclusivity when we come up with something new. That has been the case with the platinum roll, which is not actually made of platinum but is an improvement in the quality of the ceramic used to coat anilox rolls. We have been extremely secretive about this development, even installing segments of the technology on weekends so only a limited number of people in the company know how it works. I'm not one of them, though the details have been explained to me. I'm just too lazy to master the technical stuff these days.

What I can say is this new ceramic is virtually non-porous, closer to what chrome is like, such that it releases the ink in a more efficient manner. When engraved with a laser beam, the laser burns a smoother, better-defined cell in this improved material. Seen under a microscope, the cells' wall surfaces are much narrower, more uniform, and more precisely shaped. In flexographic printing the quality of the anilox roll is the most significant factor in the production of quality prints.

When we focused on how best to market this new product, we noted the color, which is different from the standard anilox roll. The original ceramic coated rolls are black. This new type has an off-black color, more of a platinum color. We decided "platinum" was going to be the name. As an anilox roll, platinum became our trademark name. Platinum™ tends to send a statement of quality, which is what we wanted.

Even though we had failed earlier to keep a manufacturing facility in Chicago going, having a plant in the Midwest continued to seem promising. That region of the country is a big market for us, the heart of the printing/packaging industry. We received some added encouragement in 1995 when committees of officials from Green Bay, DePere, and Appleton, Wisconsin flew to Charlotte to visit us and promote their individual region as the best location for our newly planned Midwestern facility. We followed up and I, along with four others in our company, went to Wisconsin in November and selected a site. We constructed a new facility and began operations in 1997.

Art Ehrenberg, who is married to our daughter Georgia, did most of the architecture and plant layout work. He spent a year putting together what he called the bible for the new operation, planning a thirty-four-thousand-square-foot facility, including the office space. Art had worked for us when we built our new facility in Charlotte and thus avoided some of the mistakes we had made earlier, like not clearly foreseeing the need for expansion. He put together a great plant in Green Bay.

When the plant was being prepared to go into operation, Georgia approached us and suggested Art be given the position of plant manager. We had not considered him for the position prior to that; we just didn't think two Charlotteans would want to live in Green Bay and raise our grandchildren up there. But they were in favor of living there and they love being in Green Bay. Art is now vice president of operations and there is no one in this company who would say he got the job because he is our son-in-law. People accept him for what he is, a very capable individual. Our Green Bay facility has become a very successful operation.

The Green Bay plant was only one of several new ventures we have undertaken in the company over the past decade. Not all of them have been as successful as that one has been.

In 1997, we made an effort to establish a manufacturing plant in South America. Earlier we had hired a young fellow, born in Mexico to Cuban parents, to be a sales representative to Latin America. He did a marvelous job selling anilox rolls, so well we had to split the territory, hiring a former boss of his to deal with the northern region.

Sales were so promising we were persuaded by our sales representative that opening a manufacturing plant in Argentina would be profitable. Our star salesman helped us to arrange a partnership with someone he knew in Argentina who had a vacant facility we could use. We were about at the point where we were going to start buying expensive equipment to install down there when the whole effort began unraveling.

It is not a story I really want to dwell on much. To put it briefly, first, personality conflicts erupted among the parties involved in Argentina. Then, when the recession hit in Argentina, it was more than they could handle. We also learned, belatedly, that Brazil has 50 percent import duties from neighboring Latin American countries, which would have given a competitor we have in Brazil a big advantage. We should have been setting up shop in Brazil. Argentina ended up being a real hassle. The entire fiasco cost us a bundle of money. We were just happy it ended before we had invested heavily in equipment. Worst of all, amidst all the conflict, we lost most of the market we had built up down there.

A few years later, we thought we could do better back in our own country because of our success in Green Bay. We bought 50 percent interest in a small competitor in Hollister, California. The partnership did not go well from the beginning. To start with, we were unable to get our partner to put much additional money into upgrading the equipment. Then, we had some differences of opinion about work habits. I don't want this to sound negative, but the California attitude versus some of the other parts of the country is different. The company had been managed relatively loosely. Folks could come and go as they pleased and nobody punched a time clock. An operator could walk up to a supervisor or manager at noon and say, "I came in at four this morning and I have my eight hours in so I'm going home." There was no way to gauge if he had actually worked eight hours.

We tried to change time schedules and some other procedures. Work would start at seven. That rule didn't go over well. Trying to change the culture from the way business had been operated to the way we operated was traumatic. We really struggled with the facility for a couple of years.

Finally, the California power problem surfaced in the summer of 2000. One afternoon our folks in Hollister received a call from the power company saying it might have to shut the power down for two hours in the afternoon. In our business, if you shut the power off, our laser equipment is shut down and everything currently going through the laser engraving process is ruined. We would have to start all over. It was the last straw. We decided we were not going to put up with all the aggravation any longer and we closed down the Hollister plant.

One more setback occurred in 2002. An Australian company with a promising new product approached us to help it with marketing. As with Harper-Love, one of our most successful ventures, these people wanted to team up with us because of our reputation for marketing and success. The company is called Opaltone, and it produced a seven-color process for flexographic printers. We formed an agreement with Opaltone in April of that year.

Unfortunately, our plans did not work out. Some of the problem, in our view, was the personalities involved, but more of the problem was just a failure to push the product aggressively. I encouraged the company to get our people much more involved in selling its product and it didn't take advantage of our skills. We still think they have a good product, a viable product for the marketplace. But after pouring so much money into the venture and not seeing the results we had been promised, we chose to withdraw from the effort. We could see no end to the red ink.

We also recently issued a license to a company we have worked with for a number of years in Bangkok, Thailand, representing our products in Asia. There is now a company called Harper Asia/Pacific that is a licensee of ours. When the company opened, all the business we had been doing in Asia and Australia was transferred to the Bangkok plant. The company is about two years old now. Having struggled with equipment problems at the beginning, it is seeing the light at the end of the tunnel and the program is beginning to move forward. It is really that company's business and its money and we earn royalties for the use of our name and for our consultation work. Given the savings in labor costs over there, teaming up with that company seemed to be a profitable way for us to stay competitive in the Asian market.

The Thais have been wonderful people to work with. We just wish they would be more aggressive in marketing. They tend to be rather secretive. They are fearful that if we announce the acquisition of new equipment or show signs of their success, their competition will find out about it. We are afraid if we don't announce it, their customers won't know about it. Tell the world what you are doing!

They bought a new, $365,000 state-of-the-art plasma flame spray piece of equipment. I wanted to make an announcement. I wanted to brag about the acquisition to the world and let people know this operation is moving forward, progressing with the latest technology. They wanted to get the equipment in, operate it for awhile, and make sure everything was perfect. I had to tell them, "Look, when you buy a machine, the market does not expect everything to be perfect on the first day. You don't set up any machine on the floor, hook it up, and it runs. All your customers know that. They buy four to five million dollar printing presses that don't just plug in and run. They go for weeks, and sometimes months, getting little bugs in the system straightened out." For us working with this company has been a lesson in cross-cultural business dealings, but it finally bought into our concept on marketing.

Here at home in Charlotte, we've had some further successes to offset our failures in Argentina and California. Our supplies division, which we started in 1971, was mostly selling a powder and liquid cleaning product, Ceramclean, for scrubbing anilox rolls between printing jobs. Up through 1999, this division generated sales of about fifteen thousand dollars a month. We began to focus more attention on that business and created a division we call Harper Scientific™. We added new product lines, from improved scrubbing brushes to instruments for evaluating the condition of an anilox roll, and did some aggressive marketing. The division will have sales this year well in excess of $1.5 million and over two million dollars next year, considering additional products in the pipeline. It is a very stable, profitable business, and is not impacted directly by the other parts of our company, even though they serve the same industry. We cannot help but grow if we make the right moves, and we have people who live or die with that business.

Our Harper Graphics Solutions™ (technical service assistance teams) are another recent venture showing considerable promise. With today's costly and increasingly technical equipment, customers often need assistance beyond what their own technical staffs can provide. We now have teams we send to the customer's plant, taking along sophisticated measuring equipment and the team's own broad experience to assist in optimizing the quality of printing a customer can achieve.

We have the most knowledgeable group of people in the world on our payroll when it comes to our market and what we do. We spend more money for these experts and we have more of them than anyone else in the world. Not only do we hire well-educated people, but we are willing to pay for them to receive additional training. It dawned on us awhile back that the smarter our employees are the better off we are going to be. And when we send people to a seminar or to take a course, they feel the company believes in them. We may run a risk that, after spending a couple of thousand dollars on people for seminars and such, they are worth more in the labor market and can find someplace else to work. Someone once said, "You can train your people and lose them, or not train them and keep them." That is a pretty profound statement to me. We have chosen to train them.

Our emphasis on having well-trained personnel is one reason our products are a little more expensive. We bring value added. If you can get by without value added, then you don't want to pay our prices. If you are truly looking for improvement and you are willing to go the extra mile, achieve the extra level, then you are better off working with Harper.

Are there other areas in which we could expand? Although we have a number of customers in Europe who have suggested we really ought to get into manufacturing over there, we have hesitated to take that step, but we are seriously considering our options as this book is being written. Europe is very competitive, and we have had our share of challenges moving into other countries. We have also discovered when we focus, we succeed; and when we go in too many different directions, we tend to be far less successful. Our market is truly the flexographic printing market, and it is a good market to be in. It is a growth market and has been for many years now.

We have had some real successes, which gives us confidence; and we have had some real failures, which tell us sometimes we are not as smart as we thought we were. We've learned the hard way to do our homework first before leaping into new ventures. We've learned there are wonderful, honest people who do not have the kind of experience, confidence, and burning desire it takes to make things happen.

These developments and the aforementioned innovations, plus considerable growth in the flexography industry, have greatly increased business for our company. We have quadrupled our overall revenues in the past ten years.

In addition, competition has also eroded prices over the same period of time. Our prices today are about 35 percent less than they were in 1990. The recession really forced the issue. And our prices are actually higher than our competitors'. A competitor is always willing to sell cheaper than Harper. But we believe our good reputation, plus the quality of our products and increased demand, keeps us growing.

These days, we really only have two major competitors. The first is Praxair. When it comes to anilox roll production, we are about the same size as Praxair (which used to be Union Carbide). Praxair is a multibillion dollar company, which includes industrial gases and many other products. Its revenue from anilox roll sales is about the same as ours. The second is Pamarco, a company that "owned" about 80 percent of the anilox roll market twenty-five years ago, but failed to continue doing what it takes to stay on top.

A number of our competitors have gone out of business in the past three years. Southern Graphics in Louisville, Kentucky, shut down, as did Consolidated Engravers in Charlotte, the company I used to work for. Fox Roller Company in Appleton, Wisconsin, has also recently closed.

Our ability to be innovative has been one key to our success in staying competitive in the industry. But success takes more than good product development. Marketing is crucial and has long been my strength. I want to focus on that subject next, along with some of the business philosophy I've developed and the management style that has worked for me.

CHAPTER FOUR

Running a Business: Our Way

As I said before, a person can build a better mousetrap, but people are not going to rush to buy it unless the new product is effectively marketed. If I have had one focus in running this company that has been an obsession for me, it is marketing. I actually love marketing and think it is key to the success of any company.

We have a marketing department of two people. Most companies the size of Harper Corporation have a marketing department of one or maybe even none. Often it is a part-time job for somebody. We have two people who work full time on marketing, handling events such as trade shows, press releases, advertising, whatever the sales department doesn't take direct responsibility for. I spend much of my time working with these two people and have not delegated marketing responsibility much beyond them.

I am always thinking of ways to increase visibility for the Harper name, in trade publications, newspaper articles, advertisements, etc. When reading trade magazines, I always look for mention of our name in connection with new developments and business trends. If I browse through a trade magazine and don't see the Harper name in there somewhere from a press release or in an advertisement, I get depressed. For me, it is imperative people be made aware that Harper is associated with quality in the printing industry.

The culture of our company is such that there are certain steps we take to address marketing and everybody understands the importance of it. Everyone pitches in. Everybody knows how we feel about our people speaking at seminars or our company personnel taking every advantage to get visibility in the marketplace, for instance, at conferences, or by writing technical articles.

Typically, in our line of business and probably most businesses, the reward an employee gets for writing a technical article and having it published is the recognition of having it published. At Harper Corporation, if you write a technical article and it is published, we give you a check for fifteen hundred dollars. A full-page ad in a trade magazine costs somewhere between three thousand dollars and seven thousand dollars to run one time. A technical article has more credibility and typically it is two to three pages long, so we gladly pay fifteen hundred dollars for it. We think it is more valuable to us than a full-page ad, and we save a lot of money in the process.

One young man working for us made close to twelve thousand dollars two years ago just writing technical articles. We were delighted. If an article is published in a magazine in Spanish, and the publication is not a major industry magazine (any foreign language magazine is not as valuable to us) we pay seven hundred fifty dollars. All English-language magazines are distributed throughout the world. We usually average an article every two or three months in trade magazines and we are known for our publishing record. This record gives us technical credibility, making us appear to be the experts since we are capable of writing about various trade-oriented subjects.

Our marketing department does a good job of keeping the company image out there. We do it better than anybody else in the industry. Keeping our name in front of the public, or at least the people in our industry, is an obsession of mine. We do this in many, many ways, and over the years we have learned how to do it better. We learned, for example, what the editors of trade journals will print and what they won't print and we seek to provide them with more of what they are look-

Ron and Katherine Harper
"I really can't remember the year this was taken, but I believe it was for a Harper brochure, or something."

ing for. When something goes right for us and we have a new development, we try to get the word out.

Even if we risk giving away trade secrets, I feel if some development is newsworthy and will give good exposure to our company, we should publish the news. This kind of aggressive marketing does expose us to the competition. They know a lot about us because we publish so much about our company. We send out press releases about what we have done or what we are doing, and we give our opinions on the technical side of the industry. As a result, we are often copied, which kind of frustrates us, but successes are frequently copied. With almost any success in the market-place, there is going to be a copycat somewhere. If others think we are making money and they can replicate what we are doing, they are going to be right in on our heels. The difference, in my mind, is we get the recognition for being the experts, the company ahead of the curve.

And we've branched out into new, nonprofit endeavors. High school and college flexo education has been a prime focus for us. We've done a lot to attract attention through contributions to educational institutions, a topic I will discuss in more detail later. We've also been success-ful at providing training and education for our customers, something we are stronger in than most companies that share our market. Flexographic printers want to know how they can improve their operations and we provide first-rate seminars to meet their need for training employees. We put considerable time and effort into this sort of endeavor, try-ing to associate Harper Corporation in the minds of those we train with top-notch products and expertise.

Even though we were not the first company to produce ceramic anilox rolls in 1972, we were the first company to *successfully market them*. That was a good example of our willingness and determination to tell the world what we had, even when others scoffed at us. Moving forward with our plan launched Harper Corporation on the road to success.

Aggressive marketing has not endeared us to our competitors. Some people view us as being arrogant. We take a lot of pride in what we do and sometime we may come across as being conceited. We boast about what we do right. We send out press releases for everything we do that succeeds; and if we fail, we just keep our mouths shut. So, we cross a thin line in the minds of some people. Whenever they turn around they are reading about Harper and all the wonderful things Harper has done. Some people resent this situation to some degree.

At the same time, there have been people who have been willing to come out and say they disliked the way we did business, but once they got to know us, they realized we are honorable and have good intentions. We try to be honest and fair. If we are perceived otherwise, those opinions arise despite our efforts to maintain our integrity.

Over the years, I have also learned we can increase sales by providing better focus for our sales staff. One way to do this is to narrow the options that are available to sell. Rather than having the salespeople offering a variety, they focus on getting a particular product sold. We have seen this tactic work well for us in a number of instances.

Early in 1990, shortly after we began producing laser-engraved anilox rolls, our salespeople could sell the customer a mechanically engraved chrome-plated roll, or a mechanically engraved ceramic-coated roll, or a ceramic-coated, laser-engraved roll. The average customer will say the price is too high no matter what, and the average salesperson who has something less expensive to offer will immediately offer the cheaper model. We were having trouble pushing the improved, better technology.

In June 1990, we discontinued producing chrome-plated anilox rolls, partly to focus the sales force on the improved technology but also because new studies had confirmed the environmental hazards associated with working with chrome. We had long used special exhaust systems to get rid of the chromium oxide fumes, and there were increasing tight restrictions on discarding the leftover waste materials. With the improved technology available, there was no need to continue working with chrome.

More significantly, in 1996, we discontinued offering mechanically engraved ceramic anilox rolls. These rolls had continued to be less expensive than the much improved laser-engraved rolls. Some people thought discontinuing the cheaper model would kill our company. But we had seen our strongest competitor, Praxair, offering nothing but laser engraved ceramics, and they continued to grow. What's more, they were dealing with the crème of the crop of the market, which was exactly where we wanted to be. My thought was as long as the salespeople had something cheaper to offer the customer, we were never really going to get moving on the laser-engraved ceramics. The strategy has worked well for us.

We saw the same kind of sales improvement when we divided our sales force into two units, one selling narrow web anilox rolls and the other selling the large web—up to twenty foot wide—rolls. The narrow rolls are produced for small presses that print labels and are as little as six inches wide. It was hard to get salespeople motivated to sell the small ones when selling the big ones seemed so much more profitable. We were losing market share with the little ones. Dividing the sales force, so some people only sell small units and others focus on selling the big ones, has worked well to reverse this trend.

My philosophy has always been customer oriented. I have tried to put myself in the customer's shoes and tried to look at what I would want if I were that person and what I would expect. I think long before it became a cliché, I had a habit of trying to *exceed the customer's expectations.*

Before we started our own company, when I was working elsewhere selling anilox rolls, I remember being instructed to pass the buck. If a customer had a problem, part of my responsibility was to convince the customer that the problem was not an anilox roll issue, not our problem, and then encourage the customer to consult its other suppliers, its ink suppliers, or its design plate people. Of course, those people would act the same way, trying to deflect responsibility. Everyone seemed to be trying to get out from under the gun themselves.

We changed that approach when we went into business for ourselves. I just did not want to operate the same way. The customer is looking for solutions, not excuses. Why not call in the customer's ink suppliers and plate suppliers and get together and try to determine what the problem is and what we might do as a group to solve the dilemma for the customer in order to make the customer's job easier. I determined we could build up a lot of goodwill if we adopted this new attitude. Responding in this way may seem like a simple notion, but we do feel like we have been exceptional.

Along these same lines, we learned early that an educated customer is easier to deal with. The more we can teach a customer about what we do, and why and how we do what we do, the easier it is to negotiate with the customer when he is drawing up specifications or determining requirements in what he wants from us. After all, we are the experts on the anilox roll side. The more we teach our customers, the less apt we are to get in trouble down the road. We have found the average customer wants to be fair and is going to give us the benefit of the doubt, but the customer has to have some knowledge to do that. Otherwise, all the customer can say is, "I have a problem and as far as I can see it is your problem. What are you going to do to solve it?"

Our response has been to lead the way in educating the industry about the technical side, through the articles we submit to trade journals and with what we call "walking seminars." These seminars offer customers and their employees an opportunity to tour our manufacturing facility and receive a full day of instruction on everything from anilox roll production to techniques for cleaning these rolls between jobs to maximize efficiency and extend the life of the roll. We also have so-called road shows, or technology displays, that we take throughout the country and set up at conferences. Our Harper Graphics Solutions division, mentioned in the last chapter, is also devoted to carrying out this educational mission. Teams will go to a customer's plant to troubleshoot problems and offer solutions.

This approach has worked well with people working in flexography, particularly with those in the packaging side of printing. These people, for the most part, are a more educated group. By more educated, I don't mean more likely to have gone to college verses just graduated from high school, but people who are better informed and eager to be more knowledgeable about the process. Less knowledgeable people, if they have a problem, assume it is our fault. We are guilty until we prove ourselves innocent. We can spend days and dollars proving it is not our fault, but we can't bill them for that. The more educated person is willing to sit down and work together toward a solution. We spend a good deal of time, effort, and money training our customers. For me it is just a fun way to do marketing and much more rewarding. I know we are good at what we do and our people are good at the tasks they perform. We try to do everything on a first-class level and we work hard at being honest and honorable.

Other elements in my basic business philosophy I've learned from motivational speakers. Dale Carnegie had an early impact on me. A lot of little lessons taught in his course have stuck with me over the years. For example, he used to say when you run into a difficult situation, look at the worst-case scenario and see if you can live with that. If you can't, then don't venture there. He illustrated the point with the story of an American who was in China when the Japanese invaded. The Japanese were coming into the little village where he was. The American said to himself, "Well, I can run and hide, and maybe escape them, but if they catch me, they will kill me; or I can stay and at least they will see I am not running and hiding, and I might stay alive." He chose to stay, and he survived. He looked at the worst-case scenario, but he knew it was certain death if he ran and they caught him.

In business, one has to put that lesson into practice when initiating new ventures, with the risks invariably involved. I've made mistakes and I think one needs to have the freedom to make mistakes if one is going to ambitiously expand. But as I have illustrated, I've also had to learn not to go too far out on a limb.

Probably the most influential motivational author for both Katherine and I was Napoleon Hill. He wrote a book that first appeared in 1937 called *Think and Grow Rich*, which was a big hit at the time and still sells well. Katherine bought the book, read it, and thought it was wonderful. At first, I wouldn't read it because the author's name sounded screwy to me and I didn't like the title. In addition, I had the fear when we first went into business that we might get rich, and I wasn't sure I could deal with being wealthy. I had no desire to be rich. I just had a desire to demonstrate my capability for running a business successfully.

Hill tells of a meeting he had when he was a young man with Andrew Carnegie, one of the leading business tycoons of the day. Carnegie, in an offhanded, casual manner, told him the secret of what had made him successful. When

Carnegie noted Hill taking what he had said seriously, he challenged Hill to devote his energies to meeting with other successful men of the time to learn from them what their secrets of success were. It is my understanding that Carnegie even arranged many of these meetings for Hill, and he challenged Hill to distill the results of his research into a book and then focus his attention on spreading those secrets of success to everyone who would listen.

In the years following, Hill met with the likes of Henry Ford, George Eastman, John D. Rockefeller, Alexander Graham Bell, and many others. He also interviewed many people who were miserable failures or settled for far less in life. Hill's book, *Think and Grow Rich*, sums up what he learned.

Reading Hill's book, I was amazed at how many of these successful entrepreneurs either started with nothing or faced considerable hardship early in their business careers. Almost to a man, Hill contends, they followed the same formula for success that Carnegie had first told him about. These were people who had a burning desire for success; they could imagine it, feel it, crave it. Through a daily habit of concentrating on what their goal was and how they were capable of achieving their goal, their whole beings became committed to the task. They then came up with intelligent plans for attaining what they sought and cultivated a persistence that would not waver when faced with adversity.

Hill's book reinforced in me the awareness that if you maintain a positive mental attitude, and just don't give up, you somehow succeed. But I understood success in a broader sense than Hill presents it. Hill speaks of working oneself into a "white heat of desire for money." For me, wealth involves much more than money, it is about riches in life, in relationships, riches in attitude. Differing from Hill, I prefer to emphasize that money should not be the primary goal of doing business. I tell young people not to worry about the money. It will come. You will be surprised.

When you do the right things consistently every day, you will receive many rewards. Money is just one of them, and not really the most important one. Still, there was much in Hill's book that I found useful.

His book was, overall, one of the most important I ever read from a business and inspirational viewpoint. Katherine was right about him and she has given fifty or more copies of Hill's book away to friends, to people starting new businesses, and to people wanting to do something different with their lives. We highly recommend the book.

With some of the men Hill interviewed there was clearly a "damn the torpedoes, full steam ahead" determination. The lesson was not lost on me. I've noted that I am not a gambling man. You won't find me at a casino. Yet in business, one does take risks. I've learned to look at the worst-case scenario and wager our chances of success. And, I've been wrong at times, and our company has paid dearly for my errors. For me such risk-taking in business ventures is not just a gamble; everything is not left up to chance. In fact, much is left up to our determination to succeed, our marketing ability, our management of people and resources, and our ability to produce a quality product. Knowing our strengths and exercising a confidence in our capabilities has been key.

There was a time when growth was everything to me, as long as we could keep our head above water. Maybe I am just a restless person. Katherine has generally been the opposite, the more conservative influence in the company. One day, our auditor, Larry Huggins of Huggins Associates, said to me in Katherine's presence, "Ron, when is enough, enough?" He was talking about growth. We have dealt with Larry for about eighteen years and have tremendous respect for him. He got through to me that day.

We spend much more time on profitability these days. I still enjoy the growth side of business, but profitability has become fun as well. This has been particularly true over the past couple of years. The economy has really gone to the devil, and some folks have had serious problems with layoffs and plant closings. A couple of years ago we had some real concerns, but we have done very well for the most part, seeing revenues increase even during the recent recession. Knowing the economic outlook and still being able to see strong balance sheets is rewarding. I now get as much joy out of profits as I used to get out of growth.

Let me add one more point regarding our business philosophy. We have always sought to be above board about everything. We have stayed away from offers of kickbacks and shady dealings. Early in our business history, we got tied in with a Fortune 500 company, doing some subcontracting for it. I recall once when a purchasing agent from this company called requesting four hundred units of some item. I priced the units and added our usual markup and said we could sell them to him for three dollars each. I was flabbergasted when this guy suggested I price the units at five dollars each, saying his company could easily afford the higher price. Then, he asked me to seal the deal by buying him a set of expensive golf clubs. Basically, he wanted to split the extra profit with us. He made us nervous and we would not complete the sale. We have never, ever done anything of the kind.

On the management and leadership side of running a business, I think I have developed my own style. My early experience supervising other people came when I was in the Marine Corps with the rank of corporal and the responsibility for directing the actions of a squad of young men. A few years later, as a twenty-five-year-old, I was managing a plant in Greenville and directing the work of fifteen men and women, plus doing other tasks. I was younger than most of my peers in the Marines and younger than almost all the workers I supervised when I was first given responsibility to manage a business. I felt my age—or lack of it—and worried about not having a higher education. Those experiences probably shaped my management style.

I have always felt one of my greatest strengths is my ability to not get overly emotional about any situation. I can sit in a meeting and listen to someone talk about something I totally, absolutely detest and disagree with; and I can calmly talk with the person about my side of the story. The other person can call me a SOB and I can sit there and be calm. Some people feel that strength in me is really a weakness, that I internalize those emotions. But I have always thought showing strong negative emotions was a sign of weakness. I don't know where I got this attitude, from my father, maybe. Staying composed has been part of my style. On the other hand, I do, internally, experience strong empathetic emotions.

I generally feel responsible for other people's feelings and well-being, and easily empathize with what they are experiencing. I usually am a tolerant and trusting person, and value harmony in relationships. Getting along with people has seldom been a problem for me. I have the reputation of being a softy to some degree. My philosophy has always been, something I learned from Dale Carnegie, to give people what I feel they deserve and then just a little more to make sure I have not cheated them. I think that approach has been true in most of my managerial relationships.

I would prefer to err on the side of thinking well of somebody who I could have reasons to have suspicions about. I want to trust you, give you the benefit of the doubt, until you prove you can't be trusted. The worst that could happen is my trust might go too far, but I would prefer to go too far and occasionally get hurt, than to distrust you until you prove you deserve my trust. That would put too much pressure on me, always to be wondering who is out to take advantage of me, or always to be wondering what people's real motives are.

There have been times when I was too trusting and too forgiving, and I've been burned. I realize many successful business managers have a much more authoritarian style, but I think in the long run my way is better. My philosophy has worked well for me.

At the same time, I am probably rather distant from most of our employees. To my knowledge, none of the employees dislike me. Many of them don't know me very well, mainly because of my obsession with being focused on the job before me. A lack of socializing is another weakness of mine.

Nevertheless, we are not real hierarchical in our company relations. I don't promote a corporate rigidity. The controller calls me Mr. Harper; the janitor may call me Ron. The general sales manager may call me Mr. Harper one day, and Ron or Mr. "H" the next day. Someone else might call me Mr. Harper but e-mail me as Ron. Katherine is more often than not referred to as Mrs. Harper or Mrs. "H."

I tend to take for granted that people will follow my leadership. And I try to lead by example more than by dictates. At the same time, I try to let people know I have high expectations of them. One of the points I've always remembered from Dale Carnegie is when he said it is important in life to give a person a reputation to live up to. I think we need to give everyone a reputation to live up to. Let our expectations be higher!

A research study was done many years ago in which a team of researchers went into a school classroom and wrote the names of all the students on slips of paper. Then they put all the children's names into a hat and randomly picked out half of them. The teacher, who was not informed about the true nature of the experiment, was told the children had been tested and it had been determined the selected children were

150

going to have difficulty in the class, and the others were going to excel. The teacher was intentionally deceived, and the children shown low expectations by the teacher as a consequence did have difficulty, while the others excelled.

The theory supported by the results of the experiment was that lower expectations get communicated in many different ways, through verbal responses and body language. A teacher may even work hard to help a child while at the same time unwittingly communicating to him that he is not expected to succeed. The outcomes can be dramatic. People tend to achieve what others expect them to achieve.

I wouldn't condone the manner in which the experiment was conducted, but from my own experience, I know how true the results are. I remember well how much difference it made in my life to have had a high school teacher who placed higher expectations on me than I was used to hearing from other people, or used to expecting from myself. This treatment made a tremendous difference at a critical stage in my life.

In managing our company, I try to put the same principle into practice. If anything, I err on the side of having too high of expectations for people. I expect people to get out of bed in the morning with a determination and drive to do something new, different, and better than the day before. I expect them to love their work and to be willing to put in long hours getting the job done. A frequent source of frustration for me, albeit a frustration I've kept hidden, has been not seeing enough of this kind of commitment. I used to be disappointed when I would go into the office on a Saturday and be one of only two or three managers there. I expected people to be more devoted to their work and to the company that is the source of their economic well being.

I'm sure I got this attitude from my mother and my father, who worked long hours; and I got it from my first real boss, Al Scala. Mom and Dad always put in long hours. Dad would work all day and then work in the store at night, sometimes staying open until midnight. The next morning, he would be up to go to his regular job. For me, a willingness to put in the hours needed is a big part of what the work ethic is about.

No doubt, employees have certain expectations of me as well, and I take those very seriously. I think that as long as employees work and do what they committed to do when they were hired, we owe it to them to be fair and to provide job security. These are obligations I have strong feelings about. I can recall being out of work with a family to feed, once because I resigned and another time because I was terminated. The experience left an indelible impression on me—it was scary as hell and left me feeling very discouraged. I remember those times when I think of our employees. A pay cut of even 5 percent is a heck of a lot of money. If you lay a person off, it is devastating.

In the thirty-three years we have been running the company, we have never had even a partial workforce layoff. We lose a few folks once in awhile. They go for more money, or they don't like their supervisor, or whatever. We've had to let a few go because of performance issues, but we've bent over backward to keep from laying people off.

My feelings about all this were put to a big test in January of 2002. We were struggling with backlog, sales, and such, and knew we were going to have to do something, either lay off a number of employees or cut wages by 5 percent. My preference was to cut wages so everybody would suffer a little bit but nobody would be devastated.

Our management team agreed. Employees were made aware of our concerns, so nothing came as a big surprise to anyone. I had expected a few complaints, but we did not get a single one. I think management and the employees were relieved all we were going to do was cut wages by 5 percent. I expected to lose a few people, but we didn't lose any.

The wage cuts were to be in effect until June 30, at which time we planned to look at our financial situation and decide whether or not to continue, or to do something different. By April 15, the situation had turned around so dramatically we told our folks we were going to reinstate the 5 percent then and not wait until June 30. By early June, the profit situation had turned around in such a positive way that the money they lost when we took 5 percent away from them we returned to them. With the people who work in production, we didn't take 5 percent away from them. We simply cut their work-week by two hours, five-percent of a forty-hour week. Even though they did not work those hours, they were paid for them in June.

When the crisis hit, I realized that if we could do something to keep everybody together, we were going to build loyalty, and we were going to have happier employees. People read about layoffs in the papers. They see their friends being laid off. I felt hanging in there together, if we could, had to do something good for both us and for them. So we did what we did. The plan made sense. And, when the turnaround came in the economy, we did not have to go looking for these people to rehire or have to train anyone new.

In the end, we earned a lot of credibility. If anyone had any doubts about our need to cut back or questioned our motives, thinking maybe Ron Harper just wanted an extra five-percent to put in his bank account, such suspicions were dispelled. Folks had to say, "Well, they were not kidding when they cut the 5 percent." People were reimbursed out of reinvigorated company profits.

With the kind of loyalty we feel toward our employees, we've never had any hint of people wanting to unionize. I've never had much sympathy for union organizers. As people say, in the 1920s and '30s, they were necessary. But I think of Cumberland, my hometown. The city used to have large companies with numerous employment opportunities. Union activities have driven them all out. The big ones are all gone. In the end, I think many people suffer as a result of unions, from everything I have seen and read.

Of course, North Carolina is virtually an anti-union state. That may be part of why we have not had any union activity. At the same time, we never crossed the line to cause folks to want to consider a union. We pay people well and treat them with dignity. In a twelve-month period an individual is going to make more money working for us. A person may make a little less an hour, but he or she will receive bonuses when the business does well. And our folks know their job security is above average.

Over the years I have assumed we are in large part responsible if we lose employees, for whatever reason, whether they resign voluntarily or we have to fire them. I get the feeling either it was our fault that we hired the wrong people in the first place, or we didn't do the right things to keep them motivated and keep them on the job. Terminating people is something we don't take lightly. I guess terminations are the most difficult task I've had to do in this business. Fortunately, it doesn't happen very often. I have always said that when the task gets easy, you are in the wrong job. Still, I do recognize when an employee's performance gets to the point where his or her presence is not good for the company, and the company's presence is not good for the employee, that person may be better off elsewhere. When we reach that point, we terminate.

I'm well aware that not all companies treat their workforce the way we do. Frankly, I have no sympathy for the crass layoff tactics some CEOs use to increase the bottom line. Nor do I think the astronomical salaries some CEOs have managed to arrange for themselves have any justification whatsoever. There are better ways to run a company.

At Harper Corporation, I've tried to manage the company differently. I've taken seriously the reputation I have, in many respects, created for myself of meeting the expectations employees have of me. For this reason, I don't think I am being too harsh to expect employees to be more committed to the company that provides them a way of life. I just wish employees would think more of how tough it is for a company to survive in today's competitive market place, how quickly everything could change for us, and how many long, long hours I put in to keep the company going strong. Maybe then they would show a greater willingness to come in on Saturday mornings or stay until 8:00 p.m. a few nights a week to make sure they do their part to keep the company competitive. Don't get me wrong, many do.

In some respects, I assume much of the credit for what has happened in this business, but the truth is, Katherine has been a partner in this business from the beginning and deserves equal credit for our success. She has some strong skills where I have weaknesses, and vice versa. We complement each other well, though we don't always see eye to eye on everything. I have been more of the initiator; she has been more of a nurturing influence, making sure things hold together. I wouldn't be where I am today without the support she has given me.

Katherine feels at times like she is following in my footsteps, when she really has been an equal. There is a tendency, where if a stranger walked in the door and wanted to speak to the top executive in the company, and Katherine and I were sitting in a room, that person would address me. I am a white male, why not? That sort of thing does happen. People don't realize how much Katherine has been a tremendous contributor in this business and a role model for me, *the fourth significant role model in my life*. She easily fits into that limited category of people who have been most influential in my life, namely, my mother, my high school typing teacher, and Al Scala, my first real boss. Katherine owns exactly 50 percent of this company. At one time she owned 10 percent. I had no problems bumping her share up to 50 percent. No money changed hands, as you can imagine. I am chairman and she is president.

We do have some general divisions of labor. When it comes to the marketing side, I am a little better at it. I get more involved in the technical side of the business, and I am more apt to formalize a training program for employees. When it comes to spending money, or making commitments on spending money in different areas, I am more likely to be the one who does it.

Katherine is responsible for the manufacturing side of the business. I used to supervise much of what goes on, but now I seldom go into the shop anymore. Katherine oversees all of the production. She is also much better than I am at attending to details. Her major contribution in the business has been making sure we don't get into serious trouble when drafting or signing contractual agreements, insurance policies, and the various employee benefits packages. When it comes to re-searching contracts, negotiating agreements, she is definitely better skilled and more patient than I am. Tasks requiring de-tailed reading, discussion, and intense consideration are not my strength. I don't enjoy sitting in long meetings talking with insurance representatives or with auditors and such. Katherine stays on top of all those particulars. Plus, if a Christ-mas party needs planning, Kat is more apt to work with a committee on the arrangements.

Our marriage has in many respects revolved around the company for the past thirty-three years, but never has the time

I devote to working been a source of contention between us. I have been more obsessed with the business, its growth, and its future, than Katherine, but that is not to say she has been disinterested. She has been supportive of most everything I have done, save for a few big exceptions.

We have had some serious disagreements. Generally, if I am feeling very committed to going ahead with a plan, Katherine may not concede, but she will back away. Other times, if she strongly objects to something that is not so important to me, I will let the matter drop. I have been the risk taker in the company; Katherine has been the more conservative influence. If somebody in the company wants to do something new and different, something a little risky, that person is more apt to come to me. I am more likely to say, "Let's give the idea a try."

With some of our ventures I have been wrong in my decisions to go ahead, and I've caught hell from Katherine for some of those failures. Maybe rightfully so because they have cost us dearly. Still, I remind myself that we would not be as capable today as we are if we had not had the learning experiences we've had due to the debacles I've gotten us into. For the most part, I think we do a rather good job, and some of our success is because we have learned from so many mistakes.

Being the more conservative influence, Katherine is usually the one who is more reluctant to take chances. She generally wants to slow down and wait. She wants to get the contract and read every word, and call the attorneys to discuss it. I usually want to talk with the people involved and if I feel I can trust them, I glance at the contract and sign it. My mode of operating may not be good, but that is the way I am. Such eagerness to move ahead has gotten me in trouble a few times. My attitude and drive has moved us forward, but Katherine's cautiousness has kept us out of serious trouble. I know I don't have a board of directors to report to, but I have a wife!

There have, however, been some exceptions to this pattern. For example, Katherine took the initiative in purchasing the needed property and getting us moving in the direction of relocating our company to its present site in 1985. I applauded her efforts. Much the same happened with our Harper-Love Adhesives new building program. We built a brand new building about a quarter mile from our corporate headquarters. Katherine dealt with the contractor and architect. I had input, but she did most of the work.

Other times, knowing she will be hesitant, I just go ahead and make a decision. In the early 1990s, I was personally involved in ordering new laser equipment. I could see the opportunities in the marketplace and, being the optimist that I am, I would order a new laser, a six-hundred-thousand-dollar to seven-hundred-thousand-dollar piece of equipment. Then I would call the bank a week or two later and say we had a laser about to be delivered and would need some money. I never had a problem with the banks; I had a good rapport with them. But Katherine would have proceeded differently. She would have called the banks first. For me, I always figured getting the banks involved early on slows down the process. When you call and tell them you have a piece of equipment on the way, that speeds everything up. It works, *if one has a clean record with the bank.*

Working together with Katherine has been much easier and more successful for me than have been our attempts to bring professionals on board to help us run the company. Looking for people to bring new ideas and concepts we were not familiar with into the company, we have hired people with MBA degrees, advanced accounting degrees, and, twice, we hired attorneys to work for us. For the most part, these people have not worked out.

From some of them I have sensed that once they learned Kat and I both received no more than a high school education, they began thinking, given their higher education and experiences at larger companies, they knew so much more than we did about running a business. They would forget that we've been in the school of hard knocks for fifty years, plus we've been married to this company for many years, and I have taken numerous business courses over the years and done substantial reading. What's more, I have a pretty good record of success as well. There is an awful lot business schools are not capable of teaching about the real world.

But no, most of these professionals have acted like, if we would just let them take over, they could take this company forward to levels of success we haven't dreamed of. We have had to explain to them we are not looking for a savior, we are not about to go bankrupt, we are not looking for a turnaround artist, we just want good, persuasive ideas that we can implement.

Had some of them come up with useful, innovative ideas, we might have thought differently. As Napoleon Hill liked to say, "You don't get paid for what you know, you get paid for what you do with what you know." Most of these guys just upset people around here and caused more problems than they were worth. One thought we needed tighter restrictions on access to upper management. He didn't think the average supervisor should be able to walk into the chairman's office or the president's office and discuss a problem concerning the parking lot or the need for some sidewalk repair or such. Katherine and I have pretty much an open-door policy. We started as a small company and we have kept some of the small-company atmosphere. This fellow thought we needed more barriers, contending such a policy would make a positive difference.

Another fellow, an attorney, thought he needed to protect us from employees who might try to take advantage of us. We also had a fellow with an MBA insist our accounting process and month-end statements needed to be sped up. In our opinion, he didn't do any better than the bookkeeper, Jean Phillips, who had been doing the accounting for us for years. One guy, a CPA, had strange work habits, staying on the job until 11:00 p.m. and not coming to work until just before noon. His schedule was not quite our work style. With one or two exceptions, including the young German fellow who has been our financial controller for a number of years now, people with advanced degrees have not demonstrated any real value to us in improving our company.

We've had better, though mixed, results in hiring our own children to work for the company. All of our children have worked for us at one point or another. Most of them started when they were young, just out of high school. Working for us was not something we pushed them to do. We did encourage it, but we didn't try to entice them into it and we never discussed with them the importance of joining the family business and eventually working their way up into positions of authority.

For them, our company was an easy place to get a job and make some spending money. If there had been a McDonald's down the street that might have been a convenient place for them to get early work experience. In this case, Mom and Dad's company was convenient. It was relatively easy to get a job and relatively difficult to get fired.

We do have regrets we did not do more to encourage our children to pursue a college education. None of our kids did. Three of them graduated from high school and two finished up by taking the GED. I've said we set a bad example for our kids there: We didn't go to college, and we have been successful. I suppose they figured they could do the same. Our children, Danny, Jimmy, Margie (married to Hal Kluttz), Chris (married to Isabela Nogueira), and Georgia (married to Art Ehrenberg), are wonderful and we love them all. Currently, Jim is vice president/chief customer officer of HarperScientific; and Margie is now the executive vice president of Harper Corporation. Art Ehrenberg, Georgia's husband, played a big role in getting our Green Bay

3 Generations of Harpers

A Commitment To Quality

Left to Right: Art Ehrenberg, Tony Ehrenberg, Jim Harper, Margie Harper Kluttz, Ron Harper, Katherine Harper, Lee Kluttz

"This is the whole family gang that works in the Harper business."

plant established and is vice president of operations for that facility. Our grandson, Lee Klutz, is manager of customer service at our Charlotte location; and another grandson, Tony Ehrenberg, is an inspector at our Green Bay facility.

For the most part, I look back over a fifty-two year career, and particularly the past thirty-three years in which we have had our own business, and feel we have exceeded our expectations many fold. The marketing strategies I have employed relentlessly, the business philosophy I stuck with, and the management style I grew into have served us well. We have gone far beyond our dreams, though I can't say we ever had long-term expectations. We used to have three-year plans and five-year plans, but never ten-year goals. Nevertheless, if I had been told thirty years ago that we would some day be where we are today, I would not have believed it.

Basically, I have lived my life believing it doesn't take a big stroke of luck for a person to succeed. What it takes is a burning desire and a willingness to put in the effort. I don't think there is anything in our lifetime we dreamed about or wanted that we don't have. Yes, I could say I wanted a jet plane some day, a dream I've let slide. If I had really had a burning desire for a jet plane, we would probably have one of those, too.

The truth is, lifestyle goals never were a big motivator for me. I was never the kind of person who would think of some luxury item I wanted and then work hard so I could have it, or buy it and then work hard to pay for it. Somehow, that approach all seems backward to me. In my view, it is easy to put the cart before the horse, to seek satisfaction in possessions rather than our own productive potential. The *doing* part, getting the job done right, far more than *having* the money and the things money can buy has been most gratifying for me. Some people may find this hard to believe. But I have just wanted the chance to work productively in a manner that gave me a sense of accomplishment. My passion for work has been satisfied and is what I have found most fulfilling in life.

The material rewards—our large, beautiful home; our weekend home on Lake Wylie; the luxury cars we drive; the luxury cruises we take; the artwork we have collected—these things can be expected to flow from a productive life, but they were never the primary objective for me. This book hasn't been about all the affluence Katherine and I have managed to acquire; it's been about my love for work. The work ethic I learned from my parents is something I have been able to live out. That, for me, is my greatest source of pride.

CHAPTER FIVE

Giving Back and the Law of Compensation

One of the greatest rewards that comes from being successful is having opportunities to give back to the community a portion of the garnered profits. Katherine and I have been able to do this and have been greatly enriched by the experience. "The harder you work, the luckier you get." I have experienced the results of following that advice. I've also learned it is true that the more you give of yourself, your time, your effort, and your dollars, the more you receive in return. The law of compensation works: The more money we give away, the more money we end up keeping. Jokingly, I have even said, "Because we are selfish, we need to give more money away."

My mother used to supervise a weekly bingo game in Cumberland, Maryland. The profits went to the local Rescue Mission to assist people who were down and out. To my mother, making a habit of contributing regularly to help others was important. Her commitment was my first experience of philanthropy work and the value stayed with me.

I have tried to continue that tradition here in Charlotte. We have contributed anonymously to a number of nonprofit groups over the years. The Charlotte Rescue Mission is one of them, along with the Salvation Army and the Red Cross. These are groups we feel have earned our respect for the work they do. We don't give huge sums, but we give regularly and when special appeals are made to help after natural disasters.

With the growing success in our business, we also found other ways to get involved in trying to influence change for the betterment of society. Getting deeply involved in the Democratic Party here in North Carolina was, for awhile, a big part of our lives. And, more recently, we have successfully worked to raise funds for and assist in the setting up of educational opportunities in the field of flexography for high school and college students.

I can't say I was politically active or even had much political awareness when I was young. My mother was a fan of President Franklin Delano Roosevelt and, along with growing up in an industrial, working-class town, her views probably influenced me to favor the Democratic Party. John Kennedy was my all-time favorite president. He had a charisma that was unique. When it came to some of the more significant political and social issues of the day, for example, the Vietnam War or the counterculture movement, I can't say I was well informed or had strong views. I was too wrapped up in my work to make the effort to understand what was going on.

As for the civil rights movement or the rise of feminism, those were issues I felt more supportive of. I have always favored equality of opportunity. I would not have the kind of work values I have, focusing on the merits of achievement and discouraging wishful thinking about windfalls of fortune, if I didn't believe everyone should be given a fair start and a level playing field.

However, it was less a concern about social issues and more a desire to get involved in the broader community to enhance our business networking that led us into politics. We had tried joining the country club, but not being golf players, we didn't find we had enough in common with other members to make our membership worthwhile. Then we asked a friend, Doris Cromartie, for suggestions. She said, "You ought to get involved in politics." My first reaction was, "Oh, my God, everyone knows politics is a negative thing."

Doris told us she would take us to Raleigh and introduce us to a few "secretaries" for a start. We went, and—this is a true story—I was expecting to be introduced to some of the typists and paper filers who work in the Capitol. She had in mind introducing us to the secretary of labor, the secretary of agriculture and the secretary of crime control. She knew these people and the governor well. During our tour of the Capitol building, this fellow came by and, seeing our little group, threw up his hands and said, "Hi, Doris." It was Governor Jim Hunt. Having never met a real live governor, I was, to say the least, impressed.

On our next trip to Raleigh, the governor invited us into his office for coffee and asked if we would mind supporting him in his upcoming bid for the U.S. Senate against Jesse Helms. Not having any idea what it would entail, we told him we would be happy to help. In the months following, we found out what is involved. It meant some real dedication, long hours, and financial contributions. That was the start for us.

We became good at hosting fund-raisers at our home. Early on, Katherine and I did much of the work, getting invitations printed, making phone calls, arranging for the catering, etc. Depending on the event, we'd charge up to two thousand dollars a plate and the profits would go into the campaign fund of the candidate we were supporting.

During Governor Hunt's run for Senate against Jesse Helms in 1984, Katherine served as Mecklenburg County financial chairman for the governor. It just so happened Sena-

1994 Ron and Katherine with good friend, Governor Jim Hunt
*"We have some very fond memories of our long association
with the governor of North Carolina."*

tor Helms's financial chairman for Mecklenburg County was
our next-door neighbor, Steve Walsh. In a funny incident, for
a fund-raiser for Jim Hunt, we had a huge tent put up in our
backyard. Katherine had to ask our neighbor if we could put
some tent pegs at the end of tielines in his yard. He said, "As
long as you let me do something when Jesse comes." A few
weeks later, he had a fund-raiser for the senator.

Over the next few years we continued to be involved. We
did fund-raisers for Eddie Knox in the Democratic gubernatorial
primary, and Rufus Edmisten in the general gubernatorial election. We supported many others on the local level. Later, we did
fund-raising for Mike Easley in his run for governor and John
Edwards when he was running for U.S. Senate.

Along the way, I was asked to serve as chairman of the
Democratic Party in Charlotte/Mecklenburg County. People

wanted to see a businessperson in the chairman's position. I had little idea how time consuming the position would be when I agreed. Honest to God, it turned out to be a full-time job. I was constantly torn between our business and trying to fulfill my responsibilities as chairman. What I did was put to work many of the same marketing strategies I had learned to employ in running a business. Overall, I think we did a pretty good job, marketing the party in the local area with television coverage, newspaper articles, and advertisements.

Then in 1986 (the same year our company sponsored the "Katherine Harper's Cleaner Hands Formula" race car in the

1985 Katherine and Ron celebrating 'Katherine Harper's
Cleaner Hands Formula' NASCAR car # 49
"Our car came in 19th place once. That is as good as it got."

NASCAR circuit), Katherine decided she was going to run for the United States Senate. I resigned my position as local chairman because I wanted to support her and I thought there might be conflicts of interest. Our tasks became magnified. We focused not just on fund-raising but also on running a full-fledged campaign. It was a fantastic experience for Katherine and a great time for me as well.

We entered the Democratic primary in the spring. Katherine announced her candidacy in January and the primary was in May. There were eight other Democratic hopefuls in the race, including Terry Sanford, former governor of North Carolina and the president of Duke University at the time. We bought a small Winnebago recreational vehicle, painted "Katherine Harper for U.S. Senate" on the sides and front, and drove all over the state. I'd drive some of the time and let others do the job when my presence was needed at home to keep the business going.

Come election time, Katherine did pretty well in the rural areas, both in the east and in the western mountains. She did less well in the metropolitan areas. She did not have the name recognition. Nonetheless, we had a marvelous experience. Terry Sanford won the primary and afterward called Katherine to ask for our support. We readily agreed and were pleased when he won in the general election. Senator Sanford became a good friend. Hanging in my office is a photograph taken in 1988 in the senator's Washington, D.C. office, with him and his wife, Margaret Rose, standing alongside Katherine and I and our two oldest grandsons, Lee and Jason.

As a result of our intense involvement, we became well known in Democratic Party circles in North Carolina and among politically minded people in general. We learned over a period of time that all politicians are not crooks. As businesspeople, we did get tired of hearing Democrats disparaging rich businesspeople, knowing how we inherited nothing and worked hard for what we have. But we gained a respect for the many people in government, both Democrats and Republicans, who really want to do a good job. True, there is a lot of bureaucracy, a lot of barriers to doing what needs to be done; nevertheless, there are a lot of wonderful and dedicated people in government who want to do what is right.

Our involvement has been a rewarding part of our lives. We have dined with governors and been to a White House reception at the invitation of President Bill Clinton. We even dined with Princess Anne of England on one occasion, at the invitation of Governor Hunt. We have a plaque on which we like to engrave the names of all the prominent political people we have entertained in our home. The only non-politician on the list is my mother, Grandma Dolly Harper, and she is there because we love her. No other non-politician appears because

To Ron & Katherine Harper
Best Wishes,

Bill Clinton

1988 Ron, President Clinton, and Katherine Harper
at a special reception for the president
"We liked this guy, and still do."

we are afraid if we start putting friends' names on the plaque, people are going to get offended because their name is not there. It's bad enough with politicians. Senator Al Gore's name is there (when he was running for president); Governor Jim Hunt's; Congressman Jim Martin's; and many others. State Auditor Ralph Campbell and North Carolina Treasurer Richard Moore are our most recent additions.

We are proud of the association we have had with politics, although we eventually curtailed our involvement because it is very time consuming. We still financially support a few candidates, but we don't get involved in the rallies, the parties, and the many other programs we used to attend.

We have a painting of the United States Capitol displayed in the conference room of our business that symbolizes for us the part we had in politics. The artist, Jim Cromartie, is the son of Doris Cromartie, the woman who first introduced us to the world of politics in North Carolina. We since learned that his great-great-great grandfather, James Hoban, designed the Capitol building in Columbia, South Carolina, then went on to design the White House in Washington, D.C., and supervised the construction of the U.S. Capitol building. Jim approached us and told us there had never been a major painting of the United States Capitol in Washington, D.C., and suggested we commission him to fill the gap. We agreed to do so in 1985, and in 1986 the finished painting was unveiled by Senator Sanford at a ceremony in the Capitol building in Washington. (The senator presented us with the U.S. flag that flew over the Capitol that day.) For the next 12 months the painting hung in Senator Sanford's office.

Since then the painting has had quite a history. At the unveiling we met the president of the United States Capitol Historical Society, who was intrigued by the claim that this was the first significant painting of the capitol building. He later had the issue researched and confirmed the claim. The

170

painting was transferred in April 1997 to Raleigh, where it was unveiled by Governor Jim Martin and hung in the state Capitol rotunda. The president of the U.S. Capitol Historical Society was in attendance to promote the historical nature of the painting.

After being on display in the state capital for a year, the painting hung in our conference room for two years. Then, in 1990, we received a phone call from the U.S. State Department saying the new ambassador to Russia, Robert Straus, wanted to borrow our painting to hang in the American Embassy in Moscow. The ambassador planned to send an airplane to Charlotte the next day to pick it up. We asked for some extra time to get some legal papers drafted. By now the work of art had taken on some value and we could imagine a few years later calling Washington and saying, "Hey, someone up there has a painting of ours." At any rate, we prepared the paperwork and a few weeks later a huge tractor-trailer pulled into our company driveway and the driver came in and said he was there to pick up the painting. He carefully wrapped it and put it in his big empty truck and hauled it away.

The painting was in Moscow for two years before being returned to us, no worse for wear. By then this work of art we had commissioned for fifteen thousand dollars was being insured by us for one hundred thousand dollars. And we started to promote it even more. We made a thousand lithograph prints of the painting and distributed them to embassies around the world. We also gave thirty-five framed copies to local Charlotte high schools. We are of proud of it and hope our kids don't sell it some day at a yard sale. The painting has some real history behind it.

Another side to politics I have taken an interest in and tried to make some contributions toward is improved race relations and equal opportunities for African Americans. Years ago, in the early 1950s, when I first went to work for Al Scala, he taught me how to do the critical job of making judgments about the printing rollers we etched. Later, Mr. Scala promoted me to a supervisory position and asked me to help select and train someone else to do the job I had been doing. I recommended a young black fellow, Robert James, because I knew he was competent. He got the job and was proud to have been selected. And he performed well.

A year or so later, I noticed he was beginning to slack off some and I asked him about it. I told him he needed to think about the possibility of future promotions, of moving up in the company. I never forgot his response. He said, "Ronnie, you know, I'm Negro; no matter what I do, I'm not really going to go anywhere in this company." Somehow, I knew he was right, and it bothered me. It went against the ethic I had been taught. People, too often, weren't just judged by their abilities and work habits. For some people, there are criteria they have no control over.

Growing up in Cumberland there was a ghetto off on one side of town that people used to call Shanty Town. Most of the town's African American population lived there. But there were some blacks who lived amongst the whites and in one of the places we lived there was a black family whose backyard backed up against our backyard. That kind of challenged some of the prejudices I may have been developing, because their backyard always looked a whole lot nicer than ours did. My mother used to say to us kids, "A nigger is a person, white or black, who is just no good. And most Negroes are not niggers."

When I moved to the South in the early 1950s, I witnessed the effects of segregation more frequently. Getting on a bus, and seeing a black person board and be compelled to go to the back and sit down was difficult for me to understand. I reluctantly accepted the situation because I didn't think there was much I could do about it. I remember the "White" and "Colored" drinking fountains, "White" and "Colored" restrooms, "White" and "Colored" schools. I can tell you from my limited experience, social and academic arrangements were not separate but equal; they were separate and unequal.

I can appreciate the consternation of African Americans at the time. I can understand why they went into Woolworth and other eating establishments and sat at the bar to be served. Katherine's father had a restaurant, and if a black person wanted food, he or she would have to go in through the kitchen. They could not be served in the front of the restaurant. That was the law. I always felt these folks deserved something better.

It used to bother me how white folks could be such good friends with black folks on an individual basis, for example, with the ladies who came to clean their homes, do the ironing, and take care of their children. They just loved them. Still, as a race, they would look down on them. And I knew whites whose attitude was, "I have nothing against them as long as they stay in their place." Some of those White folks had grown up dirt poor themselves, and I think there is some truth in the notion that it was important to them to have someone to look down on. As for many white, middle-class Southerners, they may not have altogether agreed with the segregationist policies, but they tolerated those policies. They went along with them because the practices were enshrined in the law, and they didn't think they could do much about changing the situation.

As for some of the harsher aspects of racial discrimination and segregation in the South, I can't say I was a witness to any episodes here in Charlotte. I know the police used to like to just beat the hell out of blacks if they got in trouble, but I never was witness to such beatings. To my knowledge, there never were any lynchings or KKK marches in the Charlotte area. We used to read in the newspaper about KKK gatherings in other parts of the state, but not around here.

I could appreciate what was happening when Dr. Martin Luther King Jr., began advocating doing something different in society, moving beyond policies of racial segregation. I think there have been many positive developments over the past forty years. There remains much that can be done, with both white folks and black folks needing to take responsibility.

When I became chairman of the Democratic Party in Mecklenburg County, one of the first groups that asked me to speak was the local chapter of the NAACP. Beforehand, I had become acquainted with a few members. I must say, I found going to speak to that group kind of frightening. My fears were probably provoked because speaking to them forced me to confront my own prejudices. So, I decided to be up front and honest. When I talked to the group, I told them I had always thought the NAACP was an African American equivalent of the KKK—one was as bad as the other. I had to confess I had learned some things. I then told them how my wife and I had both grown up with prejudices, and how residual prejudices can remain even if we don't consciously want them to. If I am walking down a dark street and I see a black person, a little bit of adrenaline comes to the surface— that sort of thing. I have also heard there are black folks who have the same kinds of residual prejudices regarding whites. We have to learn to try to keep our prejudices, whatever remains of them, on a conscious level, where we can work to deal with them. My plainspoken remarks earned me some friends that day.

Recently some friends from the Democratic Party asked us to host a fund-raiser for the state auditor, Ralph Campbell. We agreed, and most of the work was done by others, though the fund-raiser was held at our home. I didn't know until I answered a knock on the door the evening of the event and the person standing there introduced himself as Ralph Campbell that our state auditor is an African American. Apparently people felt no need to inform me what race the man was. To me, my first encounter with him was a sign of progress, and the way racial and social relations should be.

There remains much more to do to improve race relations in this country and to provide equal opportunities for black folks. There remains a lot of prejudice in some white communities. And there is more black folks can do to help themselves. I find it promising to hear African Americans talking less about the legacy of slavery and more about the need for educational opportunities, stable family life, and programs like the Stop the Killing, headed up by the Reverend James Barnett. I think the NAACP has got to quit worrying about how "we were slaves for four hundred years." Let's start looking more to the future, look at the opportunities we have in America, and take advantage of them. This outlook is what the NAACP has got to preach. Let's do something with our lives; let's study a little harder in school; let's work our way through adversities; let's lay claim to the American dream. That work ethic served me well; and even though some people don't always get a level playing field, I really don't think there is any viable substitute for it.

From my position, I have felt there is more I can do to help others, and where my biggest contribution has been is in helping to provide educational opportunities for students, regardless of race, who want to pursue a career in flexography. I would encourage every youngster who can to go to college and further his or her education. While I may have had no formal education beyond high school, I have taken many courses, and have read many, many books. I think I eventually made up for my lack of a college education. Nonetheless,

I think a college education would have helped me to overcome the inferiority complex I had early in my career. It would have given me more confidence as well as broader skills.

Personally, and as a company, we have been especially active in contributing to education during the past thirteen years. For us it is an ideal win-win situation. We contribute funding and materials to educational programs that teach students to be qualified workers in the flexographic industry. We benefit by getting exposure for our name and products, and by contributing to the overall growth of the industry.

In my opinion businesses ought to do more to contribute to education in this country. I'm not against grants from the government and taxpayer-supported education, but I also think the average business can do more. I actually think the average businesses, if better informed about what they can do and the benefits that can come from being involved, would be willing to contribute more. Frankly, in the past, educators have not really wanted businesses sticking their noses into something they know nothing about, namely educating young people. Attitudes are changing.

In our experience, for the most part, educators have welcomed our efforts. And it is not just the money they want. They have welcomed our time, our suggestions, our recommendations, *and* our money. Educators want to know what they can do differently to help make the education they provide more relevant to the future of their students' lives. They realize they are in the business of training young people who will eventually be in business. The overlapping interests between educational goals and business are ripe for more input and development.

Industry has some obligation in the area, in my opinion. If industry is going to generate attention and attract young people, it needs to get involved, spend the money up front. If we hire someone off the street with no knowledge of our business, we spend a long time training that person, and it can be expensive. If we can get someone else to train that person, or if the printers and converters can get the schools to train their new workers, my gosh, that is a big load of dollars off their shoulders. So why not write a check occasionally and give to the schools.

The leading technical association dedicated to development in the field of flexography, namely, the Flexographic Technical Association (FTA), based in Ronkonkoma, New York, formed a foundation in 1978 devoted to education. Katherine and I got involved in 1990, when I suggested to the executive director and president of the foundation that we raise funds to get flexography into high schools. Already, there were some good programs in a number of colleges. Clemson University, in Clemson, South Carolina; Rochester Institute of Technology, in Rochester, New York; Fox Valley Technical College, in Appleton, Wisconsin and others have led the way in providing well-trained graduates for the flexographic industry. We followed up our suggestion and co-chaired the raising of a million dollars for the foundation.

For Katherine and me, it was like being back in 1967 when we were actively involved in raising funds for the O'Donahue Catholic school library here in Charlotte. That was our first experience at fund-raising and we quickly learned we were good at it. Finding yet another good cause to do fund-raising got us all excited. We were also in a position by then to make some sizable contributions ourselves and we have done so every year since.

The movement to get flexographic training into high schools has gotten off to a great start and has spawned increased efforts on the part of many colleges to get involved as well. There are now twenty-one high schools in the United States offering training in flexography. Four of those are in North Carolina and five in South Carolina. Two such programs have also opened in Canada. Katherine and I have given most of our attention to nurturing the programs in the Carolinas, and we are currently very involved in trying to get a fifth program going in North Carolina.

One of the bigger challenges we have had to face in opening flexographic programs in high schools has been retraining the school counselors. Young people who struggle with

1990 Ron, Katherine and George Parisi, former president of the FFTA
"This was our first substantial contribution to the FFTA Flexo in Education Fund. We started giving back to an industry that has been very good to us."

their academic studies, who don't do well in math or English, for example, get shunted into the "vocational education" classes, where they are encouraged to learn to work with their hands. Just as often, it is kids with attitude problems who get moved into the graphics arts department or the shop classes. Those departments don't want all the kids with attitude problems and can't do a good job training their students if that is all they are given.

First off, schools need to and are trying to abandon the use of the term "vocational education." The term has a negative connotation, denoting a step down because such school-ing isn't college prep. In our view, this form of education is "technical training," preparing young people for viable ca-reers in business and industry. The businesses would not be supporting these programs if there was not a demand for the skills graduating students have to offer. What is being pro-moted is real-world education.

On the high school level, one purpose we had from the very beginning was to take the kind of student who was on the verge of dropping out and encourage him or her with hands-on work in flexography, working with real presses. Students can make their own designs, then work with their projects through the entire printing plate preparation and print-ing process until they see the end result, with their own de-sign printed. Some youngsters who do not perform well aca-demically excel when they have an opportunity to do practi-cal, hands-on assignments.

Once some of the struggling students get into flexography, they begin seeing the relevance of other subjects. They rec-ognize the importance of math because they have to convert dimensions from inches to microns, the standard of measur-ing used in parts of the manufacture of anilox rolls. When they begin mixing inks and learning the qualities of various inks, they begin to understand the relevance of chemistry. It is like when I was a student, I couldn't see the need for his-tory because I had no plans to be a history teacher. I wasn't sure I needed English because I wasn't going to be a writer or a reporter. What flexography can do is escalate in a youngster's mind the importance of subjects that seem like so much need-less abstraction when studied in isolation.

I've heard Thomas Edison had a heck of a time in school. He was thrown out of school a couple of times. Yet, no one doubts he had a brilliant mind. Many students are like Edison, needing a different take on learning to bring out the mental capacities they possess. The first part of our mission is to try to give students another way to learn, using a process where students can visualize the way something works and participate in using a procedure to create their own designed products. If the best we do is give those students a renewed interest that holds them in school until they graduate, we feel we have given them something important. A high school diploma can give a person much-needed positive feelings about him- or herself. Without a diploma, youngsters are often left feeling inferior to the general population, but surprisingly, thousands of students drop out of high schools every year; twenty-five thousand dropouts each year are recorded in North Carolina alone. In my mind, too many young people are being left with an inferiority complex and such feelings can all too quickly lead to other problems in their lives.

Second, our purpose has been to provide students with marketable skills they can use after they graduate and go into the workforce. Only 50 percent of students who graduate from high school go on to college, and half of those who go to college drop out before completing a degree program. We have been primarily concerned with helping students who do not choose college, by training them for positions in a growing industry.

Job prospects for ambitious students are excellent. Even in a slow economy, the flexographic printing industry continues to expand. Students graduating from FTA-funded high school programs get a head start in "flexo," being familiar with the vocabulary of the industry. Plus they have a working knowledge of the ins and outs of design work, printing plate production, anilox roll use, ink qualities, and other aspects of flexography. We don't just train them to be press operators; in fact we try not to emphasize the press-operating aspect because we want students to get a broader education that can open up a wide range of avenues for advancement in the industry. These jobs are not minimum-wage jobs, but a promising livelihood.

The flexography programs established in high schools have been an inspiration to colleges. A few colleges already had programs that were developed in response to industry demands and growth. Some of these now receive students coming out of high school flexo programs and have had to upgrade their curriculums to provide training at a higher level of technical expertise. Other colleges have jumped on board and opened up new programs. Twenty-seven colleges, including one in Canada, now offer training in flexography.

Locally, we have been very involved at the college, as well as the high school level. The southwest campus of Central Piedmont Community College (CPCC) now has the

1999 Central Piedmont Community College students
printed a label to celebrate the establishment of the
Harper National Flexographic Center (HNFC)
*"We were totally surprised by this label–**printed flexo!**"*

1999 Central Piedmont Community College, Charlotte, NC, dedicated The
Harper National Flexographic Center
"We were inspired by Dr. Tony Zeiss, president of the college."

Harper National Flexographic Center, with much thanks and credit due to Dr. Tony Zeiss, president of the college. Students can earn a two-year associate degree in flexography, learning to work with three flexo presses. CPCC also offers monthly programs and seminars that individuals can enroll in for short-term training. This curriculum is an attractive option for people already working in the industry who want to upgrade their knowledge base and skills.

Clemson University has a similar program that is even further developed. The program attracts full-time students as well as many students who come in for one week of training. They teach design for flexography, press setup, electronic image generation, ink mixing and management, preparation of photopolymer plates, anilox roll selection, and a host of other subjects people who work in flexography need to know. Most of these colleges have presses, machines we supply the anilox rolls for on request, free of charge. Clemson University has four flexo presses, including a six-color in-line press.

When we want employees at Harper Corporation to understand the complete flexographic process, we can get them trained at Clemson University, Central Piedmont Community College, or Flexo Trade School, and we are quite willing to pay for the training even though we have donated significantly to their various programs.

Our contributions to all this have gone beyond fundraising and making financial contributions ourselves. We provide any high school or college in the nation that submits a request with free anilox rolls. We've also helped with the purchasing of the Narrow Web presses, which cost, with an educational discount, around thirty-six thousand dollars. In addition, plate equipment, cleaning products, and all kinds of other items associated with such a program are needed. We have helped many schools, through the Foundation of the Flexographic Technical Association, get set up with supplies and equipment. Contributions from Harper Corporation and from us personally over the years total approximately one million dollars, which includes time, products, and dollars. We have offered assistance, as well, with curriculum development and to advise on other aspects of these programs. For this and other contributions over the past forty years, in 1999 I was elected to the Flexographic Technical Association "Hall of Fame."

Further, we don't try to hide the fact that we benefit as a company from our contributions to these educational programs. Our involvement is very much a win-win situation for us. The community wins, young people win, industry wins, and the schools win; nobody loses in this game. Harper Corporation wins because our name becomes associated closely with flexography and, in particular, anilox rolls and maintenance products in the minds of more and more people going into the industry.

Most people in this country have never heard of flexographic printing. They probably have heard about offset printing and, these days, they know about digital printing, but flexography is not a commonly used term. We aim to change this situation. Just giving recognition to students who do well in the educational programs we support spreads the word about our industry among parents and neighbors. Thousands of people become aware of flexography as a result; some even understand what makes it unique.

In the competitive standings in the printing industry flexography is well ahead in package label printing, though it still lags behind offset printing in total volume. Gravure printing has about the same market share as flexography. There have been big shifts, however, in the last ten years. Offset and gravure have lost ground to flexography. It is hard to know where the industry will be twenty-five years from now. Some people project a significant relative decline in offset printing, a significant increase in digital printing, a continuing increase in flexography, with gravure remaining about the same. Of course, there will also be growth in the entire industry as well, which will yield yet more business to printing processes that remain competitive, and flexography is very competitive. Our objective is to preach flexography and gobble up more and more market share.

Thirty years ago, flexography was a minor competitor, when the quality of offset and gravure were far superior. Flexography was cheap so it did attract a certain market, but the quality left much to be desired. But conditions have changed during the past twenty years or so. The quality of flexography can now match the standards set by other printing methods. What's more, over the long run, flexography is still less expensive. The cost of the presses can be comparable, but the operational costs are lower. That difference gives us an advantage.

Flexo is less expensive and just as good, quality-wise. We are trying to get this message out to the end users. The big food packagers, for example, we try to get them to go flexo in printing the labels that go on their products. Newspapers used to all be printed on offset presses. Currently forty-four newspapers in the United States are printed utilizing the flexographic method, including the *Charlotte Observer* and the *Raleigh News and Observer*

Our involvement in educational programs has been, from everything I've seen and heard, time, effort, and money well spent. It has been good for us, both personally and as a company. I think ultimately that the things we do for people to make a difference in their lives are the ac-

1997 Ron accepting the Governor's Award for Excellence in
Workforce Development at an annual banquet
"One of the many exciting and special occasions in my life."

185

complishments we ought to take most pride in. I honestly believe whatever we can do for others is more important than what we can do for industry, even though to some degree it is one and the same.

In addition to our contributions to high schools and colleges, we have also been honored for our donations to a couple of other institutions. There is now a Harper Flexographic Museum at Appalachian State University in Boone, North Carolina, with Dr. Mark Estepp deserving much of the credit for making the museum a reality. There is also a Harper Flexo Technology Wing at Fox Valley Technical College in Appleton, Wisconsin, thanks to Dr. Victor Baldi, the former president of the college.

The more we give the more we have left over. Financially our company is far better off today than it was in 1990, yet we have given away far more time, effort, products, and dollars in the last fourteen years than we did in the first nineteen years we were in business. The past fourteen years have been, by far, the most successful of all our thirty-three years in business. It is phenomenal. The law of compensation must have some truth to it. Give and you will receive much more in return than you have given. I now know that to be an absolute truth based on personal experience!

When we first started contributing to educational programs, we helped CPCC put a flexographic printing program into its graphics arts department, located then in the same building on Elizabeth Avenue where I started out forty years earlier as a young man working for Charlotte Textile Engravers. The college has since moved its graphics arts department to the Southwest campus on Arrowood Road. But it gave me no small amount of satisfaction to see the program start where I started, knowing the curriculum would open up opportunities for others to pursue what became my passion. I hope they will experience the satisfaction that comes with a job well done, and, perhaps, reap some of the success the printing industry has given me.

Now, if you drive into the Southwest campus, you will see a large white sign in front of one building that reads "Harper National Flexographic Center." The sign is there because of the time, effort, and dollars we have put into flexography at the community college level. To me, however, it means a whole lot more. I see more than just an educational center. I visualize my life and the role I've had in advancing flexography. And I see the promising outlook that flexography holds for students who enter the field.

Chapter Six

Reflections on Life

Ten years ago, Katherine and I, along with our friends Gerry and Pat Henke, planned a vacation in Alaska. The itinerary was to fly into Seattle then on to Fairbanks, followed by a scenic train ride to Anchorage, and a cruise along the coast of Alaska. In the weeks prior to leaving for our vacation, I worked seven days a week trying to get caught up on a backlog of work. The weekend before we took off, Katherine and I went to the office and I carried a heavy briefcase from the car into the building and down to our conference room. When I got there, I felt so exhausted I had to lie on the floor for fifteen minutes. Katherine gave me an aspirin, which made me feel better, and I kept saying to her, and to myself, that all I needed was a couple of weeks of rest and I would be fine.

A few days later, we got on an airplane and flew, first, to Seattle. When we disembarked there to change planes, I carried a small carry-on bag off the plane into the terminal and felt completely exhausted afterward. I had to sit and rest awhile. We requested an electric golf cart vehicle to transport us over to the gate where our connecting flight was departing. I continued to feel horrible that night in the hotel in Fairbanks and had serious difficulty sleeping.

The next morning I felt a little better, and we boarded the bubble-top train that would carry us from Fairbanks to Anchorage, which was about an eight-hour trip. The scenery was all lost on me because, finding the seating uncomfortable, I spent most of the trip stretched out on a metal bench back near where the train carriages were hooked together.

Katherine took charge when we reached Anchorage, saying we would drop our luggage off at the hotel and go straight to the hospital. When she informed the manager at the hotel, he personally took us to the hospital, where I was wheeled into the cardiology section of the emergency room.

After examining me, the doctor informed me I had suffered, not one, but three minor heart attacks. Fortunately, none of them were massive or I probably would not be here now. I was told immediate that bypass surgery was needed. When we discovered that only twenty-one bypass operations had been performed in the Anchorage hospital in the preceding year, Katherine told the surgeon, "We are going to take him back to Charlotte," where over two thousand such surgeries were being performed annually. I remember kidding with the doctor, telling him we had brought an extra hundred dollars with us, so we wouldn't have any problem paying his bill.

Over the doctor's objections, Katherine made arrangements to get us back to North Carolina. For the first time ever in our travels, she had purchased insurance and was therefore able to arrange a medivac airplane to fly out of Charlotte to pick us up in Anchorage. On the return I remained on my back the entire flight, hooked up to monitors and attended to by two nurses, in the executive-style jet plane. We made one re-fueling stop in Montana.

Two days after returning to Charlotte, I had surgery. I had never had surgery before and have had a fear all my life of someone cutting me. The morphine they gave me took all the fear away. The night before, during preparation for the surgery, I was told I would be taken to the operating room at 7:00 a.m. When I awoke, I asked someone what time it was and was told it was 6:00 a.m. "Well," I thought, "it's another hour before I have to go through with it." What I didn't realize was it was 6:00 a.m. the day after. All I had to do was try to move a bit and I could feel the pain throughout my upper body from an incision that went clear down my chest.

A few days later I was home from the hospital and still having a hard time sitting up without assistance. Visitors began stopping in, saying I was lucky and God was definitely on my side. Honestly, it had never occurred to me I might die, and the fact that I didn't die did not amaze me. All my life, I have never had a fear of death. Confronted with the very real possibility of it, I felt more anxious about being cut open than of dying.

Talking about death used to depress me, as when speaking with life insurance agents. That has all changed now. I have no problem these days addressing the prospect of my death, and with estate planning and general financial planning, I've even grown used to it. What I am less comfortable with is knowing that as people grow older, pain comes more frequently to the body. And for some people, ailments like dementia and other diseases affecting the elderly set in. We've watched as Katherine's brother George has slipped into dementia. Sometimes I think I would prefer to die than face what he is going through. Then, again, I wonder whether I really understand what he is experiencing. I just don't know. I do know I would not want to be a terrible burden to others and get to the point where I couldn't do anything for myself.

There have been a few other changes occurring for me since my heart attacks. For one, our diet is different these days. We try, at least most of the time, to eat a heart-friendly diet, something I was never too concerned with before. In little ways, I try to do more physical work to get some exercise. We did invest in a treadmill and a stationary cycle soon after my recovery from surgery, but all my good intentions went by the wayside. Exercise for exercise sake was not a value most people of my generation learned. Enough physical tasks needed to be done when I was a kid without a person requiring special equipment to get enough exercise. I found exercise equipment too boring.

I've learned to enjoy little physical tasks like puttering around the yard at our lakeside home, moving rocks from the front of the lot down to the bank by the lake using the battery powered wheelbarrow contraption that was a recent Father's Day gift from Katherine. I absolutely love doing that. I wash windows, hose down the porch and feed the dog, fill the dishwasher, even make the bed. I guess if we had a baby, I'd be changing diapers. I've discovered a new pleasure in such menial tasks, something I used to think I shouldn't waste my time doing because there were business books and magazines to read and business plans to be considered.

For awhile after my surgery, I tried to quit smoking. Katherine wouldn't let me smoke. I used to smoke Benson and Hedges cigarettes and gave those up. Katherine has smoked Virginia Slims ever since they came out marketed as the preferred brand for women. So, after my surgery, when I would get up at about 5:00 in the morning, I'd get out of bed on my own, go out to the kitchen, and light up one of her Virginia Slims, smoke about an inch, put it out, and place it up on the shelf. Ten minutes later, if Katherine wasn't up yet, I would get it and smoke a little more. Finally, I went and bought my own pack, but I bought Virginia Slims so if Katherine saw them lying around she wouldn't know the difference. That's how I got started smoking the "women's cigarette," and I still do.

My one big weakness is my addiction to cigarettes. I truly enjoy smoking and smoke roughly a pack-and-a-half a day. I keep telling myself I am not going to be one of those people affected by cigarettes. I do know about the health risks, however. When the no-smoking trend started, we did prohibit smoking in our whole manufacturing and office complex. Then Katherine and I began to cheat a little bit, smoking in our own offices, and everybody knows but nobody complains. Still, I can't imagine what life was like for non-smokers in the old days when people smoked on airplanes and in offices and cafeterias, even in hospital rooms.

I think I have also learned how to relax more. I used to have a hard time justifying taking a day off from the office. When my mother and father would visit many years ago, coming down to Charlotte to be with us for a week or two, I just couldn't take time off. I might go in a half-hour later, and leave work a half hour earlier, but I never took a day off. There were times I would leave early in the week on a sales trip and arrive back late Friday afternoon and go straight to the office to see what was happening, rather than calling it a week and going straight home. If I had to do life over again, I would land at the airport at 2:00 and head for home. That is what everybody else does.

The first time Katherine and I went on a cruise, I dreaded it. Five days on a ship with all those people and nothing to do but lie in the sun or read. I absolutely dreaded that. But I ended up enjoying it, and our next cruise was seven days. A ten-day cruise is the longest we have taken. We've probably been on about twenty cruises over the past twenty-five years. In that respect, I finally got to the point where I could relax and enjoy such pleasure trips, but I had to get out of town, get out of Charlotte, get out of the country.

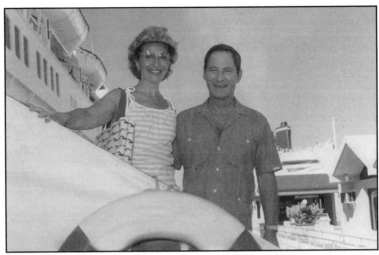

1985 Kat and Ron on a Caribbean cruise
"Even I fell in love with cruise ships!"

I have learned to enjoy travel more, and we have visited thirty-two countries during the past thirty-plus years:

Canada	Aruba	Tahiti
Mexico	Barbados	Russia
Honduras	Grand Caymans	England
Costa Rica	Jamaica	Scotland
Venezuela	Martinique	Norway
Panama	St. Croix	Finland
Colombia	St. Kitts and	Sweden
Ecuador	Nevis	Greece
Galapagos Islands	St. Lucia	Holland
(Ecuador)	St. Maartens	Denmark
St. Thomas	Puerto Rico	
St. Johns	Australia	

In addition to these, Katherine took a business trip to Paris, France, in the summer of 1981. I stayed home.

We enjoyed the experience of flying on the supersonic Concorde a number of times: once on a round-trip to London; and following a cruise from New York to South Hampton, England, on the *QE-II*, with Pat and Gerry Henke, we returned on the Concorde. We have also visited, on business or pleasure, forty-six states in the United States. Wyoming, Idaho, North and South Dakota are the only ones we have not been to.

I am ready to slow down and spend more time with Katherine. I realize neither one of us is going to live forever and we need to take advantage of our time together. And in all fairness to the employees of the company, I need to step back from some of my responsibilities at the office and let a well-trained and ambitious management staff, that is already in place, take charge. Someone else needs to be making the big decisions. They are going to make some mistakes in the process. They have certainly had ample opportunity to learn from my mistakes. Frankly, I think they are already doing a pretty good job. I sit at home and worry about them, but we are going to have a great year based on decisions other people have made. Maybe I am not the only one who can make the right decisions in the company.

I can tell you when we first started the business, I personally went to the post office, I personally picked up the mail, and I personally opened the mail. I used to get a kick out of looking at purchase orders from customers, or checks from customers, or inquiries from customers. It took me a while to relinquish that job to where somebody else picked up the mail, but I still opened it. Then, somebody else opened it, but I still read it all. Now, all I see is the junk mail. I don't even see my own personal paycheck. Those were my thrills in the early days. But I do realize time is moving on.

That said, I confess I still find I relax best when I am doing something productive. We've all heard the line about how nobody on their deathbed has ever said, "I wish I had spent more time at the office." And I can't say I have much respect for the kind of guys we sometimes read about who work like hell to get rich and die of heart attacks at age fifty. Is it really worth it? However, I don't think of the work I do as a stress-filled, anxiety-ridden, exhausting activity. I generally feel most comfortable when I am busy on a project. I am very project oriented and there is so much I want to get done. I am never caught up and as long as I am living, I will never, ever, get caught up. My work doesn't stress me out. To me work is the thrill of life. It is what keeps me going, what makes life meaningful for me.

I've also had to learn—and it took a long time—there are relatively few people who want to emulate my work habits. I know I have been referred to as a workaholic and I don't mind that title. I am not quite as bad as I used to be, but I also think workaholics are the ones who built this country. I think it is workaholics who build strong companies that provide employment for others and security for their families.

For years, I used to get depressed about more people not being in the office on Saturdays, because I came in every Saturday, and I still do occasionally come in for two or three hours on a Saturday. I thought everybody should want to work at least six days a week. To me, work was, and still is, one of life's great pleasures. I couldn't understand why others weren't eager to get to work at 7:00 a.m. and weren't willing to stay until 6:00 or 7:00 p.m. to get work done. I believed that was what people were supposed to do. It is certainly what I did all my life, and my parents did all their lives.

It took me years to understand if you are a good lathe operator, and that's what you want to be, then being a good lathe operator is the right thing to do. Thirty years ago I couldn't understand a person who was content to live his or her life without striving for the next promotion. I thought there was something wrong with people who didn't want to do more.

Then I began to understand that what all of us are really look-ing for in life is some degree of happiness for us and our families and there are different ways to attain happiness. For me it came through the challenges of the job, but I came to realize other people may experience life differently. If a per-son can clock in at seven and clock out at three-thirty, and not go the extra mile trying to make the top salary, that can be okay. As long as a person is happy and has made plans so late in life he or she can retire and not be a financial burden to somebody else, that is okay. These days, I don't mind going to the office on a Saturday morning and being the only one in the building. It is also nice when I see two or three others, and sometimes I do see others; but they do it on their own terms, never because of any pressure from me.

When I reflect on what it is that has motivated me over the years, I think one of my strengths is the ability to pat my-self on the back. Some people shun recognition, and other people are constantly seeking it. I think I am somewhere in the middle. I want it, but I can get it *from me*. If I do a job well, and I know I have done it well, I can say, "I did a good job," and I feel good about that. I don't have to have some-body else tell me how well I am doing.

In other respects, I think the motivating factors have changed over the years. Recently I dug out of the attic the love letters Katherine and I exchanged in the months after we first met and re-read some of them. That period was a very happy part of my life. I was nineteen and she was eighteen. We were so in love. Working to become financially indepen-dent, starting a family, trying to excel at work, these activities motivated me in the early years of our marriage.

Looking back now, the years seemed to pass so quickly as I threw myself into the different jobs I had. At the time, I thought I had forever. When I was twenty-five, I got bored listening to discussions about retirement and planning for a comfortable retirement. Retirement for me seemed like it was one hundred years away.

Age thirty was a difficult time for me. I had been working for eleven years and felt like I hadn't accomplished enough and was getting old. At forty, rejuvenated by our new business getting off the ground, I thought I had a long time to go. Even fifty seemed like a long way from sixty-five, which is what I thought of as being really old. The thought that my time was somehow limited didn't occur to me. At sixty I had my heart surgery and it gave me some pause. But only in the past few years, leading up to seventy, have I have been motivated more and more by thoughts of my own mortality.

At seventy-one, I realize how quickly time passes and how much I still want to accomplish. I'm prepared for my death and realize the day will come. I just hope it is later, rather than sooner, because there is so much I still want to do. Every time I get a list of projects I want to do, before the list is 25 percent complete, there is another list started. The urgency to get work done before my lifetime expires is what motivates me these days. I have to tear myself away from my computer at home late at night, sit with Katherine and have a glass of wine, and try to put my work aside, relax, and go to bed and get a good night's sleep. Early the next morning, I am up and on the computer again. There is always something more I want to get done.

I'm the kind of person who could never retire, but it doesn't mean I won't change careers. I have a fear of doing nothing; I can't imagine doing that. Whether I write a book that never gets published, or consult on marketing with companies, or do some motivational speaking, there are other things I can do. I don't think I am like my father, who had absolutely nothing he could take with him beyond the railroad and died shortly after he retired at sixty-five. He was a very important person running that big locomotive. Without his job, he had little to look forward to.

If I could have lived my life differently, I think I would have loved being a high school teacher. I'm not entirely sure why. Going to a teachers college is what I had planned to do after high school, before the U.S. Marine Corps yanked me away from my planned pursuit. Now, I think there might still be time for some teaching experience. At seventy-one years old, I have taken another public speaking course, Ty Boyd's "The Executive Speaking Institute" seminar. I do all right in front of small groups if my talk is short and sweet. More and more I'm being asked to give presentations to large groups of people. I've begun to realize people are interested in what wisdom I have gleaned from my years of devotion to building a successful company.

A second factor draws me in the direction of teaching. Increasingly, I feel I want to share with young people, my grandchildren among them, what I have learned from life and the recommendations I have to offer others who are

1993 Grandma Dolly Harper, 81 years old, with her grandchildren at our home

just getting started on the adventure of life. And since it was with my grandchildren in mind as a primary audience that I set about working on this book, I want to note at this point who they are:

Our Wonderful Grandchildren (All thirteen of them)

Name	Birth	Parent(s)
Daniel Jason Harper (Jason)	1975;	Danny
Ronald Harper Kluttz (Lee)	1975;	Margie
Christina Marie Harper (Christina)	1983;	Chris
Robert Anthony Ehrenberg (Tony)	1983;	Georgia and Art
Natalie Laine Harper (Natalie)	1985;	Chris
Lydia Nicole Kluttz (Lydia)	1985;	Margie and Hal
Londyn Michele Ehrenberg (Londyn)	1986;	Georgia and Art
Erica Ashley Kluttz (Erica)	1987;	Margie and Hal
Joshua Nathaniel Harper (Nathan)	1988;	Danny and Lynn
Benjamin James Harper (Ben)	1991;	Jim
John Alexander Harper (John)	1991;	Chris
Dylan Ehrenberg (Dylan)	1994;	Georgia and Art
Raphael Harper (Raphael)	2003;	Chris and Isabela

My advice, to begin with, is to choose a livelihood carefully and then *fall in love with your chosen career.* Like a puppy, it will return your love. A person needs to love what he or she does for a living. This is so essential. Rather than an adventure, life can degenerate into a treadmill experience if one doesn't love one's work.

Think of every morning as the start of a great day. The difference between a mediocre day and a great day is often in the mind of the beholder. Nothing in life comes easy. Don't expect it to. Nevertheless, develop a positive outlook and cultivate it. We control the interpretations we give to situations. The glass is half-full or half-empty depending on the attitude we approach it with.

Develop and nurture a good work ethic. This starts with

Summer of 2003 Dick Harper, Steve Harper, Ron Harper, and Gary Harper
"My Brothers."

loving one's work, but it includes discipline and consistency and a strong sense of pride in achievement. Stay focused. Don't be distracted by little irritants. They can sap your energy and lead to nothing being accomplished. Workaholics are simultaneously criticized and envied. Try to strike a balance in your life, but if you must err—and only if you love your work—err on the side of crossing the line to being a workaholic.

In our consumer culture, much too much emphasis gets placed on work as a means to money needed to buy material possessions, many of which are often non-essential luxury items. The desire for those things becomes the prime motive for work. I submit there is much we need to learn in order to reclaim work as having value in and of itself. Work is rewarding. Work can be fulfilling. Work gives us a sense of achievement. It is work that integrates us into a community as contributing members and makes us feel like we belong.

Work to exceed the expectations of your managers and your customers. Go the extra mile. Aim to be above average. Don't settle for less. Strive to make yourself indispensable in the workplace.

Make a point of getting along well with your fellow workers and others you cross paths with in life. A brilliant person who does not have the ability to get along with people spends a lifetime struggling to succeed, and usually jumps from job to job looking for the perfect place to work. There is no perfect company, one that is going to satisfy you all the time, just like there is no perfect marriage. If there were a perfect marriage or perfect company, you would get bored with it after awhile and you would soon part ways from it. There would be no challenge, nothing to develop your character. In that regard, it wouldn't be perfect.

Be honest. Don't cheat in your dealings with others or with the government. A reputation for dishonesty can ruin a career. Pay your taxes. If you think taxes are unfair, get involved to influence changes.

People will sometimes take advantage of your trust, but that is not the norm. Do not suspect a person of a wrongdoing until it becomes obvious that he or she should be suspected. In other words, give people the benefit of the doubt until it becomes certain they no longer deserve that benefit. Be prepared to compromise. You may feel certain of a situation, but even so, you may not always be right.

If you feel people deserve to be paid ten dollars for a job well done, give them eleven dollars, just to be sure you are fair. You will not only win their appreciation and respect, but you will also reinforce their good work habits and sense of achievement.

Don't worry about the money. It will come. You will be surprised. When you do what is right consistently every day, you will receive many rewards. Money is just one of them, and not really the most important one.

We strive for happiness all our lives. Know that money does not buy permanent happiness—and sometimes not even temporary happiness. Happiness comes from within. You can choose to be sad—or happy. You control this emotion. Control it wisely. Much too much emphasis gets placed on money as the prime measure of success and the source of happiness. I prefer to measure my success in terms of what I've been able to accomplish and how I've been able to help others through my efforts. And I know that having money beyond what is needed to take care of basic needs does not make a person happy, no matter how much a person might possess. Without the satisfaction that comes from applying oneself in creative and productive efforts, no amount of money is going to make a person happy.

The automobile that gave me the most pleasure was a thirteen-year-old Chevrolet, the first car Kat and I bought when we could barely afford it, but it was ours. The living space I have the fondest memories of was our first apartment here in Charlotte. That little place wasn't much; we couldn't afford much. But we had earned the rent money and we shared it together. It was ours—a place for us to share our happiness. Anything you gain in life that you truly work for, that you have earned, you are going to feel better about.

Give of your time, effort, and dollars to those you can help. You will be repaid many times over. You will always receive much more than you give. God just may have some influence on that phenomenon. I know our business has been most successful during the years we have given the most to educational and charitable causes. Our most meaningful rewards have been the opportunities we have had to work with others to make improvements in educational institutions and in the community. Satisfaction comes from such involvement.

As you grow older, you will realize love and a loving companion is all-important. Katherine and I have been friends from the beginning. As I often say, we are friends most of the time, and that is about the most we can hope for. At the same time, we have been loyal companions for fifty-two years. We enjoy one another's company and the activities we do together. We've learned to work around our differences and work through our conflicts.

If Katherine and I have learned anything, it is not to be angry with one another for more than fifteen minutes. One of the most miserable experiences for a married couple is to go to bed angry. We try awfully hard not to do that because we both get hurt. It is not worth it and it doesn't solve any problems. We try to get the anger out and deal with it, mainly because we value our relationship and we know there is much there that is worth preserving. Katherine and I really have been so terribly, terribly blessed in our marriage these past fifty-two plus years. I certainly have no regrets and I think I may even feel a little guilty; maybe that is why we spend so much time paying back, so to speak.

I do believe there is a God. I believe there is an afterlife and it is better than life here on earth. But spirituality has not been the kind of intense experience for me that it is for Katherine, though there is one exception to that, and this may sound strange. I have learned from Katherine that during an airline flight when the air turbulence gets to be severe—something that makes me very uncomfortable—if one asks St. Anthony for help, the turbulence quickly settles down. I've witnessed the effectiveness of this enough times to start really believing it. Most of the time Katherine is with me, so I don't have to do the praying, she does it.

For the most part, however, I am more of a "God helps those who help themselves" kind of person. The idea that, for some mysterious reason, God has chosen to bless me with success in ways he has chosen to not bless other people, and I therefore should be grateful to him for undeserved fortune, is not a notion I dwell much on. I just can't imagine God being more generous to me than to somebody else. Such divine capriciousness, blessing some people and not others, sounds too much like luck to me. I think I am more apt to just accept life as it is and recognize the fact that it wasn't intended to be easy. I also think adversity is good for us; I truly think it builds character. My worldview and my work ethic have focused much more on the understandable: We can improve our station in life through consistent, disciplined work habits, and we are much better off if we take this approach rather than wait for some big stroke of luck or divine intervention.

Sometimes I sit and ponder the many things Katherine and I have done and the many places we have been, the numerous people we have met, and I am just in awe. We have traveled and visited virtually all over the world, something we didn't dream of doing years ago. We talk about Harper Asia Pacific, located in Bangkok, Thailand. We discuss our sales reps in Latin America, in Europe, and in Australia. For a kid who grew up in little ol' Cumberland during the Depression years, every once in a while, I just can't believe it. I think, how wonderful our lives have been.

I think of what we have been able to do for others, especially in light of the little we had when we started. The day we married, we had the clothes on our backs, our faith, and our love—and that was about it. Neither Katherine nor I had a job. (She had just resigned from the Bank of Charlotte and I had been discharged from the Marines twelve days prior to our wedding.) We've been employing over two hundred people in Harper Corporation of America and Harper-Love Adhesives Corporation combined. We have been able to positively influence those people's lives and the quality of life they have been able to enjoy. We've offered job security and provided them with health insurance. We've enabled them to send their children to college. I think that is important and I am proud to have been able to do my part to make it all happen.

Driving up toward our company's headquarters after nineteen years of it being in its current location, and seeing what is there, gives me a feeling of accomplishment. I find it unfortunate that money is considered as the first measure of success in the minds of most people. *There is so much more to life than money.* The important questions for me are: Have I made a difference in this world? And have I had a substantial positive influence on someone's life over the past seventy-plus years? *I pray I have.*

Following is a beautiful poem I learned in the ninth grade. It has stayed with me for fifty-seven years. I would like to think it is an appropriate ending for this book.

ABU BEN ADAM
By James Leigh Hunt (1784-1859)

Abu Ben Adam, may his tribe increase
Awoke one night from a deep dream of peace
And saw, within the moonlight of his room
Making it rich, like a lily in bloom
An angel writing in a book of gold.
Exceeding peace had made Abu Ben Adam bold
And to the presence in his room he said
'What writest thou?'
The vision raised its head
And with a look of all sweet accord answered:
The names of those who love the Lord.
"And is mine one?' said Abu.
"Nay not so' replied the angel
Abu spoke more low
But cheerily still and said
'I pray thee then write me as one that loves his fellow-men'

The angel wrote and vanished.
The next night it came again with awaking light
And showed the names of whom love of God had blessed.
And lo! Ben Adam's name led all the rest.

Afterword:

Since starting this book in May 2003, Katherine and I have virtually semi-retired. The young (at least younger than me) managers began taking over the reins at Harper in August 2003. Katherine and I are still involved, but considerably less on a daily basis.

The management group has performed at the early stages far beyond my expectations. Despite my earlier reservations about doing so, the group prepared the groundwork for expanding further into the European market. In April of 2004, we reached an agreement with a German company to begin jointly manufacturing and marketing Harper's proprietary Platinum™ Anilox Rolls, as well as HarperScientific™ Supply Products and Harper GraphicSolutions™ Consulting Services. This new venture, "Harper Graphics, a Harper/Inometa Company," has already begun marketing our products throughout Europe, as well as the Middle East and Africa. A complete manufacturing operation is being setup in Germany and will begin producing Platinum™ Anilox Rolls in 2005.

We are grateful for the many wonderful employees who have helped build Harper Corporation into a successful global organization over the past 33 years.

We are fortunate to have so many good friends inside and outside our business.

We are very grateful to have been born in the United States of America.

Katherine's and my marriage is more wonderful and loving than ever.

We are very proud of our children and our grandchildren.

Just recently, I received an invitation from the principal of Allegany High School in Cumberland, Maryland, where I graduated in 1950. I've been informed that I was selected as a charter member of the Allegany High School Hall of Honor, recognizing "those whose success in their chosen career has brought dignity and pride to our school." Who would have guessed fifty-four years ago.

Then, on May 3, 2004, the Board of Trustees of Central Piedmont Community College, in Charlotte, passed a special resolution proposed by our good friend Dr. Tony Zeiss. Dr. Zeiss had submitted a proposal to rename the seventy-nine acre Southwest Campus the "Harper Campus." This campus houses the Harper National Flexographic Center and hosts the annual International Phoenix Challenge High School Flexo Competition. CPCC serves over 70,000 full-time and part-time students. Katherine and I are proud to be associated with this wonderful educational institution.

Also included in the proposal, and accepted by the Board, were provisions for the establishment of a scholarship fund in the name of Ron and Katherine Harper. Preferences will be given to students studying flexography, as well as those needing special financial assistance, and to Harper Corporation employees and their children.

Truly, God has been good to us.

As I put the final touches on this manuscript on May 12, 2004, just prior to publishing, I readily admit that *Life is still beautiful*!

Ron Harper